D1443775

# macaron
# f.e.t.i.s.h

## 80 Fanciful Shapes, Flavors, and Colors to Take Macarons to the Next Level

Skyhorse Publishing

# TABLE OF

‘Macaron Fétish
- it's love
at
first bite ’

‘Macaron
Fétish
- C'est
l'amour
dès la
première
bouchée ’

## 1 Let's Get Started

## 2 Classique . Classic

## 3 Exotique . Exotic

# CONTENTS

# Let's Get Started

Growing up in Malaysia, I was surrounded by cuisines from different ethnic backgrounds in my daily life. In such a multicultural country, the national cuisine is really a melting pot where many cultures and exotic flavors come to mix and blend together.

After my arrival in France, I finally had a taste of French pastries and have to admit it was love at first bite. My passion for baking finally had a chance to blossom. My father-in-law is a great baker, and I am lucky to be able to learn from him.

The very first macaron I ever tasted was a chocolate macaron. A crispy shell with a yummy filling that melted in my mouth—what else could someone with a sweet tooth ask for but a Parisian macaron?

So there I was in 2009, setting off with strong determination to attempt my first macaron. After all, it couldn't be harder than baking a chiffon cake, right? Wrong! I got a full tray of flat, ugly, rough cookie look-alike macarons! Devastated, I had quickly given up the thought of ever baking them again.

Thanks to the encouragement from my husband and after hours of researching many blogs and recipes, batches and batches of eggs gone into the garbage, and countless failures, my very first batch of macarons with feet was born! I was overjoyed and jumping up and down in the kitchen like a little girl who just found a box of hidden chocolates.

I must admit that I have a love–hate relationship with macarons. There were days when I stuck my nose in front of the oven to look for the glorious macaron feet only to find flat or cracked cookies in the oven.

I created my blog Macaron Fetish in 2010 when I joined up with other macaron fetish bloggers in MacTweet to share the joy of baking these jewels with endless imaginable colors and flavors.

In this book, I aim to share my recipes with other bakers—from simple classic to sophisticated flavors. I have worked, experimented,  and concentrated on diverse flavors and exotic ingredients, ultimately binding the taste of East and West together, just as in the diversity of Malaysian and French cuisines.

I hope you will enjoy the journey to discover macarons as much as I have.

Let your imagination go and have fun!

*Happy Macaroning,*

*Kim H. Lim-Chodkowski*

## Oven & Baking Tray

Regardless of the model or type, the most important thing is to get used to the oven you have. You may have to adjust the temperature and baking time by a few degrees and minutes, respectively.

## Digital Scale

The dry-to-wet proportion in making macarons is crucial, so a precise digital scale is ideal.

## Food Processor & Sieve

To get a smoother and finer dried mixture, a food processor is a must to mix the almond flour and powdered sugar into a fine mixture. A sieve helps to remove any impurities that might cause bumpy macaron shells.

## Candy Thermometer

A candy thermometer is useful to determine the exact temperature of the sugar syrup when making buttercream or Italian meringue.

## Electric Hand Beater / Stand Mixer

If you have a stand mixer, you'll have the advantage of having free hands while beating the egg whites. If you're using a hand beater, use a circular motion and increase the speed slowly. Use a faster speed at the end until the egg whites form firm peaks.

## Silicone Spatula

Spatulas are used for "macaronage" (the folding of dried ingredients into the peaked egg whites). The silicone spatula is more flexible and thus allows the mixture to be folded and mixed thoroughly without breaking too many egg white bubbles.

## Piping Bag & Plain Round Tip

For standard macarons of 1 1/2 inches (4cm), tips of 8mm–10mm can be used. A smaller and finer nozzle is also useful to decorate the shells. In this book, a No. 8 tip, for example, has an 8mm opening.

## Parchment Paper

Use only nonstick parchment paper. It will help you detach the macaron shells easily when they're cooled.

## Almond Flour

Because store-bought almond flour is great and widely available in the baking section of the grocery store, there's no need to grind almonds at home. If you can't find it, buy sliced or slivered blanched almonds, and use a food processor to grind them further into powder form.

## Sugars

Powdered sugar is used to mix with the almond flour, and superfine (or castor) sugar is used to make the meringue.

## Food Coloring

Powdered food coloring is better than liquid because it doesn't add any moisture to your macaron mixture. If not available, paste or liquid food coloring can be used in small quantities. The liquid form will result in a paler end color.

## Egg Whites

Aged egg whites form peaks and make beautiful, firm meringue. I usually prepare the egg whites a day in advance and let them sit at room temperature in an airtight container until the next day. Egg whites can be stored in an airtight container in the refrigerator for up to seven days.

## Baking Chocolate & Heavy Cream

High-grade baking chocolate from a professional store is ideal for making chocolate ganache to fill macarons. Not only is it less sweet, it's also better in quality and taste. Only heavy cream is used to make a chocolate ganache because its higher fat content (35 percent) gives it a nice consistency.

## Butter & Egg Yolks

These are the key ingredients to make buttercream.

## Little Fantasies

Candied flowers, dried petals, grains, sugar pearls, and many decorations found in the baking section will make your macaron fetish fantasies come true.

## Fruits, Flavorings, Jams, Spices

Apart from chocolate ganache, you can spice up your macaron fillings with any imaginable flavor. Just let your creativity go and have fun exploring.

Getting It Right

Trial and error is the best way to discover what works and what doesn't. There's no secret—a successful batch of macarons depends strongly on two particular factors: macaronage and your oven settings.

* Start with a small quantity. My recipe uses only one egg white to minimize waste should the macarons not turn out right. To bake more macaron shells, simply multiply the quantity.

* When beating your egg white, add only half of the superfine sugar into the frothy egg white. Continue to beat by slowly increasing the speed to maximum for around 2 minutes. Add the rest of the sugar and continue until stiff peaks form. The meringue should be smooth and shiny.

* When mixing the dry ingredients into the meringue (macaronage), the first few strokes should be done with a stronger motion to break down some bubbles in the meringue. After that, slowly fold the mixture using a "lift-turn-fold-press" motion. Slowly pressing the mixture at the end of each fold binds the dry ingredients to the meringue. When you get a smooth and shiny mixture, stop folding, and lift the mixture with the spatula. It should fall back slowly like lava into the bowl, but it should not be runny. You could also check the lines formed from the lifted mixture: They should disappear slowly within 30 seconds. Only then is the mixture ready for you to pipe. Do not overfold because it will become too runny and very difficult to pipe.

* Tap the bottom of the baking tray with your hand to flatten out the macarons slightly. Let them sit for about 30 minutes. Try touching the macarons softly when the time is up. They should form a "skin" but not stick to your finger. If they do stick, prolong the time by 10-minute intervals, and check again. The length of time necessary will depend on humidity.

* Preheat your oven to 300 °F (150 °C), heating from the top only if possible. When the oven is ready, put your macarons on the bottom shelf. Bake for 6 minutes, checking to see if the feet have started forming. Open the oven door slightly, and close it back quickly. This will allow humidity to escape. Change the heating setting to bottom only, and set the timer for another 6 minutes. Increase the temperature to 320 °F (160 °C). This will help in cooking the macarons and further rising of the feet.

* Make sure the macarons are completely cooled before removing them. You could wet your working area and slide the baking sheet over it to speed up the cooling process, but do not let it sit there for too long, or else the macaron shells will become soggy.

Q : My macaron cracked.

A : 1. The oven was too hot. Try reducing the heat by 20 °F (10 °C), and prolong the baking time by 4 minutes.

2. The macaron is underfolded. Please refer to "Getting It Right" on page 6.

Q : My macaron is dome-shaped or flat with no feet.

A : If your macaron is dome-shaped and rough on the surface, the mixture is underfolded. If it's flat, it's overfolded. Knowing when to stop folding is the key to getting those pretty little feet. Please refer to "Getting It Right" on page 6.

Q : My macaron shells stick to the baking sheet.

A : The macaron shells are underbaked. If they are still stuck to the baking sheet after they have cooled down, put them back in the preheated oven at 300 °F (150 °C), and bake for another 2 to 4 minutes.

Q : I can't seem to get the macarons to be the same size.

A : On one side of the parchment paper draw some circles measuring 1 1/2 inches (4cm). You could use a small glass to do so. Leave about an inch of space between each circle. When you turn the parchment over, you will be able to use the circles as a guide.

Q : My oven has no heating option for only top or bottom.

A : Try using convection heating and lower the temperature to 285 °F (140 °C). At the end of the day, it depends on how hot the oven is because some ovens seem to heat up more than others. Give it a few tries and note the process.

Q : I cannot find food coloring in powder form.

A : Use food coloring in either paste or liquid form. Mix it in after your egg white has formed stiff peaks. Then, add your dry ingredients and start folding the mixture. Use only a small quantity of the liquid food coloring, and please note that it will appear much paler after baking. Another great option is to use icing food color powder/paste or gel food coloring.

Q : My white macarons did not turn out white.

A : Commercial bakeries use titanium oxide as a white coloring agent to make macarons white, but any white coloring might help. Alternatively, you could use white powder coloring, but in my personal experience, the macarons will look more ivory than white. Pale-colored macarons tend to turn brown when baked. Lowering the oven temperature by about 20 °F (or 10 °C) and increasing baking time will help.

# recette de base

## {the basic recipe}

1 large egg white (40g)

2 1/2 tbsp (30g) superfine sugar

1/3 cup (30g) ground almonds

1/3 cup + 4 tsp (50g) powdered sugar

1/2 tsp powdered food coloring

(to add to dry ingredients)

or

1/4 tsp gel/paste food coloring

(to add to stiffened egg white)

Get your tools ready. Put the tip in the piping bag, and stuff a part of the bag into it.

Beginners should place the bag over a container and secure the opening. This makes pouring the mixture into the bag easier.

Finely blend the almond flour, powdered sugar, and food coloring. Shift into a bowl and set aside.

With a hand beater, beat the egg white until frothy. Slowly incorporate half of the superfine sugar. Beat until the egg white forms soft peaks.

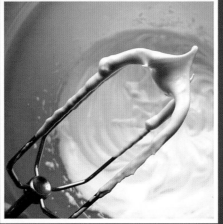

Add in the other half of the sugar, and continue beating until the egg white forms stiff peaks. The egg white should hold up like a bird's beak.

This is how a stiff-peaked meringue should look—smooth and shiny.

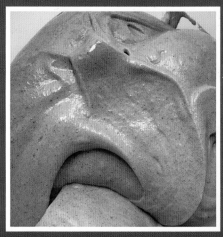

Add the dry ingredients and start folding gently. This should take 50–60 strokes, using the "lift-turn-fold-press" motion.

The mixture is ready when it flows like lava, and makes a thick ribbon when lifted. It should also sink back slowly.

The mixture should be smooth and shiny. Any lines created when lifting it should disappear within 30 seconds.

Pour the mixture into the prepared piping bag. Pull out the tip, and slowly press down the bag. Twist the top of the bag, and start piping onto parchment paper lined over a baking tray.

Gently press the piping bag. Then, release the pressure and make a quick swirl to finish. Repeat until all of the mixture is used up. Tap the bottom of the baking tray to release any large air pockets in the macarons.

Let the piped shells sit for 30 minutes. Preheat the oven to 300 °F (150 °C). Put the macarons in the oven and bake for 10–15 minutes. Let the shells cool off before removing them from the paper.

Makes 48 macaron shells | 30 minutes drying time | 12–15 minutes baking time

## Shells

......................................................................................................

* 2 egg whites (room temperature)
* 3/4 cup + 4 tsp powdered sugar (100g)
* 2/3 cup (60g) almond flour
* 1/3 cup (60g) superfine sugar
* 1 tsp red powder food coloring
* 1 tsp yellow powder food coloring
* 1 tsp blue powder food coloring

## Tools

* Baking tray lined with parchment paper
* Big piping bag with a tip No. 8 placed inside
* 3 small freezer bags, folded at the bottom up to the side and stapled to make a piping bag
* 1 big and 2 medium mixing bowls
* 3 rubber spatulas

## Methods

......................................................................................................

* Put the almond flour and powdered sugar in a food processor. Blend them finely, sift, and set aside.
* With an electric beater, beat the egg whites, starting at low speed and increasing slowly to maximum until frothy.
* Add in half of the superfine sugar, and continue to beat at maximum speed for around 2 minutes. Add in the other half of the sugar, and continue to beat until the egg whites form stiff peaks.
* Mix the dry ingredients into the egg whites. Just roughly combine them because they will be separated into 3 parts later.
* Divide the mixture into 3 parts, and scoop out 1/3 of the mixture for each extra mixing bowl.
* Add the yellow powder food coloring into one bowl, and start folding until the mixture becomes smooth and shiny. Repeat for the other 2 parts with the red and blue powder food coloring. For complete folding tips, please refer to the picture guide on page 11.
* Fill each freezer bag with each color. Snip off the head of each one, and carefully place all 3 bags inside the big piping bag.
* Pipe your mixture onto the parchment paper on the baking sheet, and let the macarons sit for about 30 minutes.
* Preheat your oven to 300 °F (150 °C), using top heat only. Place the macarons on the bottom shelf, and bake for 12 minutes. Touch a shell softly. When the macaron doesn't slide on the feet, it's baked. Let the macarons cool down before removing them from the oven.

When the egg whites form stiff peaks, fold the dry ingredients into them.

Roughly combine them. Do not fold the mixture completely because it will be separated into 3 parts later for coloring.

Divide the mixture into 3 parts - Scoop out 1/3 of the mixture for each extra bowl prepared earlier.

After each mixture is colored and folded, fill each freezer bag with a separate color. Snip off the head of each freezer bag.

Carefully place all 3 bags inside the big piping bag with the tip. You might want to readjust accordingly, so that all 3 bags contain about the same amount, so the separate colors flow out equally during the piping process.

Preheat the oven to 300 °F (150 °C). Put the macarons in the oven for 12 minutes. Let the shells cool off before removing them from the baking sheet.

classique

{classic}

Makes 24 macaron shells of 1 1/2 inches (4cm)
Preparation : 30 minutes drying time
Cooking time : 12–15 minutes baking time + 45 minutes to prepare the filling

## Ingredients

### For the shells:

* 1 egg white (40g)
* 2 1/2 tbsp (30g) superfine sugar

* 1/3 cup + 4 tsp (50g) powdered sugar
* 1/3 cup (30g) almond flour
* 1/2 tsp unsweetened cocoa powder

### For the filling:

* 1.75 oz (50g) dark chocolate (finely chopped)
* 3 1/2 tbsp (50g) heavy cream (35% fat)

## Methods

### For the shells:

* Follow the basic macaron baking methods on pages 8–11.
* Sprinkle some cocoa powder over the piped shells.
* Bake at 300 °F (150 °C) for 12 minutes. Let the macaron shells cool down before removing them from the baking sheet.

### For the filling:

* Add the cream to the pot, and warm it over medium heat until it starts to boil. Remove from the heat.
* Place the chocolate in a heat-proof bowl, and melt it over water bath. When chocolate is melted, remove it from the water bath. Be careful to wear protective gloves, as the steam is very hot and could burn your hands.
* Pour the cream over the chocolate 3 times, mixing well with a hand whisk after each addition. The ganache should be smooth and shiny.
* Transfer the chocolate ganache to a small bowl, and cover it with cling wrap touching the ganache. Set in the refrigerator for 1 hour until it is slightly thickened.
* Proceed to piping. Keep the macarons in an airtight container in the refrigerator.

Makes 24 macaron shells of 1 1/2 inches (4cm)
Preparation : 30 minutes drying time
Cooking time : 12–15 minutes baking time + 45 minutes to prepare the filling

## Ingredients

### For the shells:

* 1 egg white (40g)
* 2 1/2 tbsp (30g) superfine sugar

* 1/3 cup + 4 tsp (50g) powdered sugar
* 1/3 cup (30g) almond flour
* 1/2 tsp unsweetened cocoa powder

### For the filling:

* 1.75 oz (50g) milk chocolate (finely chopped)
* 2 1/2 tbsp (40g) heavy cream (35% fat)

## Methods

### For the shells:

* Refer to the basic macaron baking methods on pages 8–11.
* Bake at 300 °F (150 °C) for 12 minutes. Let the macaron shells cool down before removing them from the baking sheet.
* When the shells are cooled, wet a small brush slightly, dip into white powder food coloring, and paint over the shells.

### For the filling:

* Add the cream to the pot, and warm it over medium heat until it starts to boil. Remove from the heat.
* Place the chocolate in a heat-proof bowl, and melt it over a water bath.
* Pour the cream over the chocolate 3 times, mixing well with a hand whisk after each addition. The ganache should be smooth and shiny.
* Transfer the chocolate ganache to a small bowl, and cover it with cling wrap touching the ganache. Set in the refrigerator for 1 hour until it is slightly hardened.
* Proceed to piping. Keep the macarons in an airtight container in the refrigerator.

Makes 24 macaron shells of 1 1/2 inches (4cm)
Preparation : 30 minutes drying time
Cooking time : 12–15 minutes baking time + 45 minutes to prepare the filling

## Ingredients

### For the shells:

* 1 egg white (40g)
* 2 1/2 tbsp (30g) superfine sugar

* 1/3 cup + 4 tsp (50g) powdered sugar
* 1/3 cup (30g) almond flour

* silver powder food coloring

### For the filling:

* 1.75 oz (50g) white chocolate (finely chopped)
* 4 tsp (20g) heavy cream (35% fat)

## Methods

### For the shells:

* Refer to the basic macaron baking methods on pages 8–11.
* Bake at 300 °F (150 °C) for 12 minutes. Let the macaron shells cool down before removing them from the baking sheet.
* When the shells are cooled, moisten a small brush slightly, dip it into silver powder food coloring, and paint over the shells.

### For the filling:

* Add the cream to the pot and warm it over medium heat until it starts to boil. Remove from the heat.
* Place the chocolate in a heat-proof bowl, and melt it over a water bath.
* Pour the cream over the chocolate 3 times, mixing well with a hand whisk after each addition. The ganache should be smooth and shiny.
* Transfer the chocolate ganache to a small bowl, and cover it with cling wrap touching the ganache. Set in the refrigerator for 1 hour until it is slightly hardened.
* Proceed to piping. Keep the macarons in an airtight container in the refrigerator.

Makes 24 macaron shells of 1 1/2 inches (4cm)
Preparation : 30 minutes drying time
Cooking time : 12–15 minutes baking time + 45 minutes to prepare the filling

## Ingredients

### For the shells:

* 1 egg white (40g)
* 2 1/2 tbsp (30g) superfine sugar

* 1/3 cup + 4 tsp (50g) powdered sugar
* 1/3 cup (30g) almond flour
* 1/4 tsp green powder food coloring

### For the filling:

* 3 1/2 tbsp (50g) heavy cream (35% fat)
* 1.4 oz (40g) white chocolate (finely chopped)
* 0.5 oz (10g) pistachio nuts

## Methods

### For the shells:

* Refer to the basic macaron baking methods on pages 8–11.
* Bake at 300 °F (150 °C) for 12 minutes. Let the macaron shells cool down before removing them from the baking sheet.
* When the shells are cooled, moisten a small brush slightly, dip it into green powder food coloring, and paint over the shells.

### For the filling:

* Add the cream to the pot, and warm it over medium heat until it starts to boil. Remove from the heat.
* Place the chocolate in a heat-proof bowl, and melt it over a water bath.
* Pour the cream over the chocolate 3 times, mixing well with a hand whisk after each addition. The ganache should be smooth and shiny.
* Grind the pistachio nuts in a food processor to a fine powder. Add it into the chocolate mixture and mix well.
* Transfer the ganache to a small bowl, and cover it with cling wrap touching the ganache. Set in the refrigerator overnight.
* The next day, whip up the ganache until stiff peaks form.
* Proceed to piping. Keep the macarons in an airtight container in the refrigerator.

Makes 24 macaron shells of 1 1/2 inches (4cm)

Preparation : 30 minutes drying time

Cooking time : 12–15 minutes baking time + 45 minutes to prepare the filling

## Ingredients

### For the shells:

* 1 egg white (40g)
* 2 1/2 tbsp (30g) superfine sugar

* 1/3 cup + 4 tsp (50g) powdered sugar
* 1/3 cup (30g) almond flour
* 1/2 tsp unsweetened cocoa powder

### For the filling:

* 1 tsp instant coffee
* 1.75 oz (50g) dark chocolate (finely chopped)
* 3 1/2 tbsp (50g) heavy cream (35% fat)

## Methods

### For the shells:

* Follow the basic macaron baking methods on pages 8–11.
* Sprinkle some instant coffee over the piped shells.
* Bake at 300 °F (150 °C) for 12 minutes. Let the macaron shells cool down before removing them from the baking sheet.

### For the filling:

* In a small pot, warm up the cream and instant coffee, and bring to a boil.
* Remove the pot from the heat. Pour the contents over the chopped dark chocolate.
* Stir and mix until a shiny and smooth consistency is obtained.
* Let it cool, and refrigerate until it sets slightly before piping onto the macaron shells.

Makes 24 macaron shells of 1 1/2 inches (4cm)
Preparation : 30 minutes drying time
Cooking time : 12–15 minutes baking time + 45 minutes to prepare the filling

## Ingredients

### For the shells:

* 1 egg white (40g)
* 2 1/2 tbsp (30g) superfine sugar

* 1/3 cup + 4 tsp (50g) powdered sugar
* 1/3 cup (30g) almond flour
* 1/2 tsp unsweetened cocoa powder

* 1/4 tsp instant coffee
* a few drops of water

### For the filling:

* 1 tsp coffee extract
* 1 egg yolk
* 3 tbsp (40g) butter (room temperature, cut into small cubes)
* 1/4 cup (30g) powdered sugar
* 2 tsp (10g) water

## Methods

### For the shells:

* Follow the basic macaron baking methods on pages 8–11.
* Bake at 300 °F (150 °C) for 12 minutes. Let the macaron shells cool down before removing them from the baking sheet.
* Mix the instant coffee with a few drops of water. Dip a brush into the mixture and paint the shells.

### For the filling:

* Add the water and sugar to the pot and heat. Place a candy thermometer into the sugar mixture.
* Place the egg yolk into a mixing bowl. When the temperature of the syrup reaches 230 °F (110 °C), start beating the egg yolk with an electric or stand mixer.
* When the temperature of the syrup reaches 250 °F (120 °C), reduce the speed and slowly pour the syrup into the egg yolk.
* Continue to beat the mixture for about 5 minutes until the mixture has cooled down.
* Add in the butter one piece at a time, and beat until a smooth consistency is obtained.
* Lastly, add in the coffee extract, and mix well.
* If the buttercream has softened up, place it in the refrigerator for a while to firm up the texture before piping.

Makes 24 macaron shells of 1 1/2 inches (4cm)

Preparation : 30 minutes drying time

Cooking time : 12–15 minutes baking time + 45 minutes to prepare the filling

## Ingredients

### For the shells:

* 1 egg white (40g)
* 2 1/2 tbsp (30g) superfine sugar

* 1/3 cup + 4 tsp (50g) powdered sugar
* 1/3 cup (30g) almond flour

### For the filling:

* 1 vanilla bean (seeds removed)
* 1.75 oz (50g) white chocolate (finely chopped)
* 1 1/2 tbsp (20g) heavy cream (35% fat)
* 1 vanilla bean or 1/2 tsp vanilla extract

## Methods

### For the shells:

* Follow the basic macaron baking methods on pages 8–11.
* Bake at 300 °F (150 °C) for 12 minutes. Let the macaron shells cool down before removing them from the baking sheet.

### For the filling:

* Pour the cream and vanilla seeds into a small pot. Warm it up, but do not boil.
* When the cream is warm enough, pour it over the chopped white chocolate.
* Mix until a smooth consistency is obtained.
* Add in the bean or extract. Mix well.
* Pipe filling onto shells.

Makes 24 macaron shells of 1 1/2 inches (4cm)
Preparation : 30 minutes drying time
Cooking time : 12–15 minutes baking time + 45 minutes to prepare the filling

## Ingredients

### For the shells:

* 1 egg white (40g)
* 2 1/2 tbsp (30g) superfine sugar

* 1/3 cup + 4 tsp (50g) powdered sugar
* 1/3 cup (30g) almond flour
* 1/2 tsp unsweetened cocoa powder

* ground hazelnuts

### For the filling:

* 1 1/2 tbsp (10g) ground hazelnuts
* 1.4 oz (40g) dark chocolate (finely chopped)
* 3 1/2 tbsp (50g) heavy cream (35% fat)

## Methods

### For the shells:

* Follow the basic macaron baking methods on pages 8–11.
* Sprinkle some ground hazelnuts over the piped shells.
* Bake at 300 °F (150 °C) for 12 minutes. Let the macaron shells cool down before removing them from the baking sheet.

### For the filling:

* Toast the hazelnuts until they become fragrant.
* In a small pot, warm up the cream until it boils.
* Remove the pot from heat, and pour the contents over the chopped dark chocolate.
* Stir and mix in toasted hazelnuts, until a shiny and smooth consistency is obtained.
* Cool and refrigerate until it sets slightly before piping onto the macaron shells.

# exotique

{exotic}

Makes 24 macaron shells of 1 1/2 inches (4cm)
Preparation : 30 minutes drying time
Cooking time : 12–15 minutes baking time + 25 minutes to prepare the filling

## Ingredients

### For the shells:

* 1 egg white (40g)
* 2 1/2 tbsp (30g) superfine sugar

* 1/3 cup + 4 tsp (50g) powdered sugar
* 1/3 cup (30g) almond flour
* 1/4 tsp red powder food coloring

* dried hibiscus petals

### For the filling:

* 2 tsp (30g) unsweetened coconut milk
* 2.1 oz (60g) white chocolate
* Dried hibiscus petals
  (see glossary pages 198–199)

## Methods

### For the shells:

* Follow the basic macaron baking method on pages 8–11.
* After the shells are piped, break the hibiscus petals into small pieces, and sprinkle them on one side of the shells.
* When the macaron shells are baked, pour 1/4 tsp red powder food coloring on a small plate. Add 2–3 drops of water.
* Blend the coloring together with a brush and paint over the other side of the shell without the petals.
* Leave the shells to cool off to room temperature before removing them from the baking sheet.

### For the filling:

* Chop the white chocolate into small pieces, and add to a heat-proof bowl.
* Add the hibiscus petals and coconut milk to a small pot. Warm over medium heat to infuse the flavors.
* When the mixture is warm, pour it over the white chocolate, and mix well with a hand whisk.
* Set aside and cool to room temperature for 1–2 hours until the chocolate ganache is slightly hardened.
* Fill the macaron shells and enjoy!

Makes 24 macaron shells of 1 1/2 inches (4cm)

Preparation : 30 minutes drying time

Cooking time : 12–15 minutes baking time + 25 minutes to prepare the filling

## Ingredients

### For the shells:

* 1 egg white (40g)
* 2 1/2 tbsp (30g) superfine sugar

* 1/3 cup + 4 tsp (50g) powdered sugar
* 1/4 cup (20g) almond flour
* 1 tbsp (10g) black sesame seeds

* 1/4 tsp green powder food coloring

### For the filling:

* 2 tbsp (30g) heavy cream (35%)
* 2.1 oz (60g) white chocolate
* 1 tbsp matcha green tea powder
  (see glossary pages 198–199)

## Methods

### For the shells:

* Follow the basic macaron making method on pages 8–11. Blend the black sesame seeds, almond flour, and powdered sugar.
* When the shells are baked, pour the green powder food coloring onto a small plate.
* Wet a brush, blend the coloring together, and paint over the center of the shell.
* Leave the shells to cool to room temperature before removing them from the baking sheet.

### For the filling:

* Chop the white chocolate into small pieces and add to a heat-proof bowl.
* In a small pot, mix the cream and green tea. Let it infuse for 10 minutes.
* Over medium heat, slowly warm up the matcha mixture.
* Pour the warm cream mixture over the white chocolate, and stir with a hand whisk until everything is well incorporated.
* Set aside to cool to room temperature before refrigerating for 1–2 hours until the chocolate ganache is slightly hardened.
* Fill the macaron shells and enjoy!

Makes 24 macaron shells of 1 1/2 inches (4cm)
Preparation : 30 minutes drying time
Cooking time : 12–15 minutes baking time + 25 minutes to prepare the filling

## Ingredients

### For the shells:

* 1 egg white (40g)
* 2 1/2 tbsp (30g) superfine sugar

* 1/3 cup + 4 tsp (50g) powdered sugar
* 1/3 cup (30g) almond flour
* 5 dried chrysanthemums (see glossary pages 198–199)
* 1/4 tsp yellow powder food coloring

* 2–3 dried chrysanthemums (remove the petals to decorate the shells)

### For the filling:

* 3 1/2 tbsp (50g) heavy cream (35%)
* 1.75 oz (50g) dark chocolate
* 5 chrysanthemum flowers
* 4 tsp (20g) heavy cream

## Methods

### For the shells:

* Blend the chrysanthemum flowers, almond flour, powdered sugar, and food coloring. Sift the mixture to remove any impurities.
* Follow the basic macaron baking method on pages 8–11.
* Sprinkle the piped shells with chrysanthemum petals.
* Bake the macarons, and let the shells cool to room temperature before removing them from the baking sheet.

### For the filling:

* Chop the dark chocolate into small pieces, and set aside.
* In a small pot, mix 3 tbsp of cream and the chrysanthemum flowers.
* Over medium heat, slowly boil the mixture. The petals will soak up the cream.
* Remove from the heat, let sit for 10 minutes, then strain over a sieve, and press to get the maximum cream. Discard the petals.
* The pressed-out cream should be 3–4 tsp (15–20g). Depending on how much liquid cream is obtained from the previous step, add in the extra cream to get a total of 2 1/2 tbsp (40g) cream.
* Put the cream back over slow heat to warm it up lightly, then pour over the dark chocolate. Stir and incorporate well.
* Set aside to cool to room temperature for 1–2 hours until the chocolate ganache is slightly hardened.
* Fill the macaron shells and enjoy!

Makes 24 macaron shells of 1 1/2 inches (4cm)
Preparation : 30 minutes drying time
Cooking time : 12–15 minutes baking time + 45 minutes to prepare the filling

## Ingredients

### For the shells:

* 2 egg whites (80g)
* 1/3 cup (60g) superfine sugar

* 3/4 cup + 4 tsp (100g) powdered sugar
* 2/3 cup (60g) almond flour

* 1/2 tsp purple powder food coloring
* 1/2 tsp yellow powder food coloring

### For the filling:

* 1/4 cup (70g) heavy cream (35% fat)
* 3.2 oz (90g) milk chocolate
* A few drops of caramel flavoring

* 1/4 tsp agar-agar powder (see glossary pages 198–199)
* 6 passion fruit

## Methods

### For the shells:

* Follow the multi-colored macaron baking methods on pages 12–13.
* Bake at 300 °F (150 °C) for 12 minutes. Let the macaron shells cool down before removing them from the baking sheet.

### For the filling:

* Chop up the milk chocolate, and put it in a heat-proof bowl.
* Bring the cream to a boil in a small pot.
* Pour it over the chocolate, add in the caramel flavoring, stir, and make sure everything is well incorporated.
* Set aside, let cool to room temperature, and cover with cling wrap touching the ganache before setting it in the refrigerator for 2 hours.
* Scrape out the passion fruit pulp, and press it against a sieve with a spoon to extract the juice.
* Pour the obtained juice into a small pot, add in the agar-agar powder, stir, and bring it to a boil for 2 minutes over medium heat. Stir continuously.
* After 2 minutes transfer the jelly onto flat plates (you may need a few plates to get a very thin jelly).
* Let cool to room temperature, and place it in the refrigerator.
* Cut the jelly into small rectangles. Pipe the chocolate ganache on a macaron shell, place the jelly over it, and squeeze a pea-size ganache on top. Close with another shell.

Makes 24 macaron shells of 1 1/2 inches (4cm)
Preparation : 30 minutes drying time
Cooking time : 12–15 minutes baking time + 30 minutes to prepare the filling

## Ingredients

### For the shells:

* 1 egg white (40g)
* 2 1/2 tbsp (30g) superfine sugar

* 1/3 cup + 4 tsp (50g) powdered sugar
* 1/3 cup (30g) almond flour
* 1 tsp Szechuan pepper (see glossary pages 198–199)
* 1/4 tsp red powder food coloring

### For the filling:

* 2/3 cup (75g) raspberries (frozen/fresh)
* 2 tbsp (25g) superfine sugar
* 1/4 tsp cornstarch
* 1/4 tsp agar-agar powder
* 1/2 tsp lemon juice

## Methods

### For the shells:

* Follow the basic macaron baking methods on pages 8–11.
* Sprinkle some Szechuan pepper over the piped shells.
* Bake at 300 °F (150 °C) for 12 minutes. Let the macaron shells cool down before removing them from the baking sheet.

### For the filling:

* Mix the raspberries, sugar, cornstarch, and agar-agar with an immersion blender.
* Filter the mixture over a small pot with a sieve to remove any impurities.
* Warm over medium heat while stirring the mixture constantly with a hand whisk for 2 minutes.
* Remove from the heat, and mix in the lemon juice.
* Transfer to a plate, and refrigerate for 30 minutes.
* Fill the macaron shells. These macarons are best eaten the next day because they may soak up the humidity from the cream.

Sweet & Peppery :
Szechuan Pepper & Raspberry Cream

Makes 24 macaron shells of 1 1/2 inches (4cm)

Preparation : 30 minutes drying time

Cooking time : 12–15 minutes baking time + 45 minutes to prepare the filling

## Ingredients

### For the shells:

* 1 egg white (40g)
* 2 1/2 tbsp (30g) superfine sugar

* 1/3 cup + 4 tsp (50g) powdered sugar
* 1/3 cup (30g) almond flour
* 1/2 tsp unsweetened cocoa powder

* dried flower petal mix (found in health stores or online)

### For the filling:

* 1.75 oz (50g) dark chocolate (finely chopped)
* 1/3 cup + 1 1/2 tbsp (100g) heavy cream (35% fat)
* 1 chai tea bag (see glossary pages 198–199)

## Methods

### For the shells:

* Follow the basic macaron baking methods on pages 8–11.
* Sprinkle some flower petals over the piped shells.
* Bake at 300 °F (150 °C) for 12 minutes. Let the macaron shells cool down before removing them from the baking sheet.

### For the filling:

* Add the cream and tea bag to a pot, and bring to a boil. Remove from the heat, and let it infuse for 10 minutes.
* Place the chocolate in a heat-proof bowl, and melt the chocolate over a water bath.
* After 10 minutes, remove the tea bag, and squeeze out any remaining cream soaked up by the tea bag. You should get 3 1/2 tbsp (50g) of cream.
* Pour it over the chocolate 3 times, whisking and mixing well with a hand whisk after each addition. The ganache should be smooth and shiny.
* Transfer the chocolate ganache to a small bowl, and cover it with cling wrap touching it. Refrigerate for 1 hour until it is slightly hardened.

Makes 24 macaron shells of 1 1/2 inches (4cm)
Preparation : 30 minutes drying time
Cooking time : 12–15 minutes baking time + 45 minutes to prepare the filling

## Ingredients

### For the shells:

* 2 egg whites (80g)
* 1/3 cup (60g) superfine sugar

* 3/4 cup + 4 tsp (100g) powdered sugar
* 2/3 cup (60g) almond flour

* 2 tsp black coloring powder
  OR
  1/2 tsp black gel coloring

### For the filling:

* 1 egg yolk
* 1/4 cup (60g) salted butter (room temperature)
* 2 tbsp (25g) sugar
* 1 1/2 tsp (8g) water
* 5 tbsp (45g) black sesame seeds
* 2 tbsp (18g) white sesame seeds

## Methods

### For the shells:

* Follow the multi-colored macaron baking methods on pages 12–13.
* Bake at 300 °F (150 °C) for 12 minutes. Let the macaron shells cool down before removing them from the baking sheet.

### For the filling:

* Dry-roast the black sesame seeds in a pan until fragrant, stirring constantly. Remove and crush with a mortar and pestle.
* Repeat for the white sesame seeds, but do not crush them. Set aside.
* Cut the butter into small cubes and let it soften up at room temperature.
* Add sugar and water to a small pot, and cook over medium heat.
* Heat until the syrup reaches 245 °F (118 °C) when checking with a candy thermometer.
* Start beating the egg yolk with a hand mixer in a mixing bowl when the syrup reaches 237 °F (114 °C).
* Once the syrup reaches 245 °F (118 °C), remove from the heat, and slowly pour it down the side of the bowl while beating the egg yolk at medium speed.
* Keep the mixer turning until the mixture temperature becomes lukewarm.
* Add in butter one piece at a time, and beat until well incorporated after each addition.
* Fill the macaron shells, and roll them over the bed of white sesame seeds.
* Let the flavors infuse for 24 hours. These macarons are best enjoyed the next day.

Makes 24 macaron shells of 1 1/2 inches (4cm)
Preparation : 30 minutes drying time
Cooking time : 12–15 minutes baking time + 1 hour to prepare the filling

## Ingredients

### For the shells:

* 1 egg white (40g)
* 2 1/2 tbsp (30g) superfine sugar

* 1/3 cup + 4 tsp (50g) powdered sugar
* 1/3 cup (30g) almond flour
* 1/2 tsp green food coloring powder

### For the filling:

* 1–2 pandan leaves
  (see glossary pages 198–199)
* 1 1/2 tbsp (25g) coconut milk
* 2 tsp (10g) water
* 1/4 tsp agar-agar powder

* 2 tbsp (25g) dark palm sugar
  (see glossary pages 198–199)
* 1 tbsp (15g) water

* 1 tbsp (15g) superfine sugar
* 1 1/2 tsp (8g) water

* 1 egg yolk
* 1/4 cup (60g) butter
  (room temperature, cubed)
* 4 tbsp coconut flakes

## Methods

### For the shells:

* Follow the basic macaron baking methods on pages 8–11.
* Bake at 300 °F (150 °C) for 12 minutes. Let the macaron shells cool down before removing them from the baking sheet.

### For the filling:

* To prepare the pandan jelly, put pandan leaves, coconut milk, and water in a deep container, and blend everything with an immersion mixer. Filter the mixture through a sieve. Pour it into a pot, add the agar-agar powder, and cook over medium heat, stirring continuously. Just as the mixture boils, set a timer to 2 minutes. Continue stirring. Remove from the heat, and pour into a shallow bowl immediately. Let it cool to room temperature before putting it in the refrigerator.
* To make palm sugar syrup, add the dark palm sugar and water to a small pot. Cook over medium heat for about 5–8 minutes until thickened. Set aside.
* Put the superfine sugar and water in a pot, and cook over medium heat until the syrup reaches 245 °F (118 °C); use a candy thermometer to check. Start beating the egg yolk with a hand mixer in a mixing bowl as soon the syrup reaches 237 °F (114 °C).
* Once the syrup reaches 245 °F (118 °C), remove from the heat, and slowly pour it down the side of the bowl while beating the egg yolk using medium speed. Keep the mixer turning until the mixture has cooled down slightly. Add in butter one piece at a time, beat, and incorporate well after each addition.
* Lastly, pour in the palm sugar syrup and the coconut flakes. Mix well until a smooth buttercream is obtained.
* Fill a macaron shell with the buttercream, cut a small piece of pandan jelly, place it on the buttercream, and press it down lightly before closing up with another shell.

Makes 24 macaron shells of 1 1/2 inches (4cm)
Preparation : 30 minutes drying time
Cooking time : 12–15 minutes baking time + 45 minutes to prepare the filling

## Ingredients

### For the shells:

* 1 egg white (40g)
* 2 1/2 tbsp (30g) superfine sugar

* 1/3 cup + 4 tsp (50g) powdered sugar
* 1/3 cup (30g) almond flour

* 1/2 tsp red food coloring powder

### For the filling:

* candied ginger (cut into small, thin slices)
* 1/2 tsp orange blossom water
* 1–2 drops vanilla extract

* 1 egg yolk
* 1/4 cup (60g) butter (room temperature)
* 2 tbsp (25g) superfine sugar
* 1 1/2 tsp (8g) water
* 1 tbsp orange blossom water

## Methods

### For the shells:

* Mix and fold the wet and dry ingredients roughly, scoop out 1 tbsp of the mixture, and put it into a spare bowl. Add in red powder coloring, and mix well.
* Fold the white mixture in the main bowl following the instructions on pages 8–11. Pour the white and red mixture alternately into a piping bag.
* To make heart-shaped macarons, pipe half of the heart by simply pressing the piping bag and then releasing the pressure while dragging towards the pointed end. Repeat for the other half.
* Bake following the instructions on pages 8–11.

### For the filling:

* Mix the orange blossom water and vanilla in a bowl, and add the candied ginger to soak them in the liquid.
* Put the superfine sugar and water into a pot, and cook over medium heat. Cook until the syrup reaches 245 °F (118 °C); check with a candy thermometer.
* Start beating the egg yolk with a hand mixer in a mixing bowl as the syrup reaches 237 °F (114 °C).
* Once the syrup reaches 245 °F (118 °C), remove from the heat, and slowly pour down the side of the bowl while beating the egg yolk using medium speed. Keep the mixer turning until the mixture has cooled down slightly.
* Add in the butter one piece at a time; beat and incorporate well after each addition. Lastly, pour in the orange blossom water, and mix well until a smooth buttercream is obtained.
* Fill a macaron shell with the buttercream, press a small piece of candied ginger on top, and close with another shell.

Makes 24 macaron shells of 1 1/2 inches (4cm)
Preparation : 30 minutes drying time
Cooking time : 12–15 minutes baking time + 25 minutes to prepare the filling

## Ingredients

### For the shells:

* 1 egg white (40g)
* 2 1/2 tbsp (30g) superfine sugar

* 1/3 cup + 4 tsp (50g) powdered sugar
* 1/3 cup (30g) almond flour
* 1/4 tsp red food coloring powder

### For the filling:

* 1.75 oz (50g) white chocolate (finely chopped)
* 4 lychees in syrup
* 1 tbsp (15g) rose water
* 6–8 frozen or fresh raspberries (cut in half)

## Methods

### For the shells:

* Blend the almond flour, powdered sugar, and food coloring.
* Follow the basic macaron baking method on pages 8–11.
* Bake at 300 °F (150 °C) for 12 minutes. Let the macaron shells cool down before removing them from the baking sheet.

### For the filling:

* Chop up the lychees into small pieces, squeeze out as much juice as possible, and pass through a sieve. Set aside. (Too much liquid will make a runny ganache, which will soften and wet the macaron shells).
* Cook the chopped lychees over low heat in a small pot for 1–2 minutes.
* Add the rose water, and warm it slightly.
* Remove from the heat. Finally, add the white chocolate, and stir until melted and well mixed. Let cool.
* Fill one macaron shell with the ganache, top up with half a raspberry, and close with another macaron shell.

Makes 24 macaron shells of 1 1/2 inches (4cm)
Preparation : 30 minutes drying time
Cooking time : 12–15 minutes baking time + 25 minutes to prepare the filling

## Ingredients

### For the shells:

* 1 egg white (40g)
* 2 1/2 tbsp (30g) superfine sugar

* 1/3 cup + 4 tsp (50g) powdered sugar
* 1/3 cup (30g) almond flour
* 1/4 tsp purple food coloring powder
* Earl Grey tea bag (to sprinkle)

### For the filling:

* 1.75 oz (50g) dark chocolate (finely chopped)
* 1/3 cup + 1 1/2 tbsp (100g) heavy cream (35%)
* Earl Grey tea bag

## Methods

### For the shells:

* Blend the almond flour, powdered sugar, and food coloring.
* Follow the basic macaron baking method on pages 8–11.
* Cut open the tea bag and sprinkle the contents over the piped shells.
* Bake at 300 °F (150 °C) for 12 minutes. Let the macaron shells cool down before removing them from the baking sheet.

### For the filling:

* Pour the cream into a small pot, and warm it up lightly. Remove from the heat.
* Drop in the tea bag, and let it infuse for 10 minutes.
* After 10 minutes, remove the tea bag, and rewarm the infused cream.
* When the infused cream is warm enough, remove from the heat. Filter the mixture through a sieve. You will need 3 1/2 tbsp (50g) of the mixture.
* Pour over the chocolate, and stir until a smooth consistency is obtained.
* Let cool to room temperature, and chill to set the ganache a little before filling the macarons.

Makes 24 macaron shells of 1 1/2 inches (4cm)
Preparation : 30 minutes drying time
Cooking time : 12–15 minutes baking time + 1 hour to prepare the filling

## Ingredients

### For the shells:

* 1 egg white (40g)
* 2 1/2 tbsp (30g) superfine sugar

* 1/3 cup + 4 tsp (50g) powdered sugar
* 1/3 cup (30g) almond flour
* 1 tsp (5g) dried coconut flakes
* 1/2 tsp white food coloring powder

* coconut flakes to sprinkle

### For the filling:

* 2 1/2 tbsp (30g) superfine sugar
* 1 tbsp (16g) water

* 1 egg yolk
* 1/4 cup (60g) butter (room temperature, cubed)
* 4 tbsp coconut flakes

## Methods

### For the shells:

* Follow the basic macaron baking methods on pages 8–11.
* Sprinkle the coconut flakes on the piped shell before baking.
* Bake at 300 °F (150 °C) for 12 minutes. Let the macaron shells cool down before removing them from the baking sheet.

### For the filling:

* Put the superfine sugar and water into a pot, and cook over medium heat until the syrup reaches 245 °F (118 °C) when you check it with a candy thermometer. Start beating the egg yolk with a hand mixer in a mixing bowl as soon as the syrup reaches 237 °F (114 °C).
* Once the temperature of the syrup reaches 245 °F (118 °C), remove it from the heat, and slowly pour down the side of the bowl while beating the egg yolk using medium speed. Keep the mixer turning until the mixture has cooled down slightly. Add in the butter one piece at a time; beat and incorporate after each addition.
* Lastly, add in the coconut flakes. Mix well until a smooth buttercream is obtained.
* Fill a macaron shell with buttercream, and top with another shell.

fruité

{fruity}

Makes 24 macaron shells of 1 1/2 inches (4cm)

Preparation : 30 minutes drying time

Cooking time : 12–15 minutes baking time + 45 minutes to prepare the filling

## Ingredients

### For the shells:

* 2 egg whites (80g)
* 1/3 cup (60g) superfine sugar

* 3/4 cup + 4 tsp (100g) powdered sugar
* 2/3 cup (60g) almond flour

* 1/4 tsp yellow food coloring powder
* 1/4 tsp orange food coloring powder
* 1/4 tsp green food coloring powder

### For the filling:

* 1 lemon
* 1 lime
* 1 orange (organic/untreated)

* 3.5 oz (100g) white chocolate (finely chopped)
* 1 tbsp (15g) heavy cream (35% fat)
* 2 tsp (10g) lemon juice
* 2 tsp (10g) lime juice
* 2 tsp (10g) orange juice

## Methods

### For the shells:

* Follow the multi-colored macaron baking methods on pages 12–13.
* Bake at 300 °F (150 °C) for 12 minutes. Let the macaron shells cool down before removing them from the baking sheet.

### For the filling:

* Wash the fruits and dry them well.
* Grate the zest of the lemon, lime, and orange. Set aside.
* Melt the chocolate over a water bath.
* Add the cream to a pot, and warm over medium heat. Stir until it comes to a boil.
* Pour it  over the chocolate 3 times, mixing well after each addition. Add the lemon juice, lime juice, orange juice, and the zests prepared earlier together.
* Transfer into a small bowl, and let cool to room temperature before refrigerating for 2 hours.

Makes 24 macaron shells of 1 1/2 inches (4cm)
Preparation : 30 minutes drying time
Cooking time : 12–15 minutes baking time + 30 minutes to prepare the filling

## Ingredients

### For the shells:

* 1 egg white (40g)
*2 1/2 tbsp (30g) superfine sugar

* 1/3 cup + 4 tsp (50g) powdered sugar
* 1/3 cup (30g) almond flour
* 1/4 tsp blue food coloring powder

* 1/2 tsp metallic lilac food coloring powder

### For the filling:

* 2 oz (60g) blackberries (fresh or frozen)
* 1/2 tsp lemon juice
* 1/4 tsp cornstarch
* 1 1/2 tbsp (20g) superfine sugar
* 1/4 tsp agar-agar powder

## Methods

### For the shells:

* Follow the basic macaron baking methods on pages 8–11.
* Sift metallic lilac food coloring powder over the piped shells.
* Bake at 300 °F (150 °C)  for 12 minutes. Let the macaron shells cool down before removing them from the baking sheet.

### For the filling:

* Blend the blackberries, lemon juice, sugar, and cornstarch.
* Pass the mixture through a sieve to remove any impurities.
* Pour the mixture into a pot, add the agar-agar powder, and heat it up over medium heat, stirring constantly. Once it starts to boil, set a timer for 2 minutes. Keep stirring while the mixture is boiling.
* Remove from the heat, and pour into a small bowl immediately.
* Let it cool to room temperature before refrigerating for 1 hour.
* Fill the macaron shells. These macarons are best eaten within 24 hours.

Makes 24 macaron shells of 1 1/2 inches (4cm)
Preparation : 30 minutes drying time
Cooking time : 12–15 minutes baking time + 30 minutes to prepare the filling

## Ingredients

### For the shells:

* 1 egg white (40g)
* 2 1/2 tbsp (30g) superfine sugar

* 1/3 cup + 4 tsp (50g) powdered sugar
* 1/3 cup (30g) almond flour

* 1/2 tsp purple food coloring powder

### For the filling:

* 1 1/2 tbsp (25g) heavy cream
* 1.75 oz (50g) white chocolate (finely chopped)
* 1/4 cup (37g) blueberries

## Methods

### For the shells:

* Fold the dry ingredients into the stiff-peaked egg white, and scoop 1 tbsp of the mixture into a small bowl.
* Add the purple food coloring powder to the main bowl. Fold until the mixture flows like lava.
* Pour the purple mixture into a piping bag, and pipe it onto a sheet of parchment.
* Dip a chopstick or toothpick into the white mixture, and slowly add a few drops of it over each piped shell.
* To make a swirl pattern, push the chopstick lightly into the piped shells, and draw the white part outwards to the purple part.
* The 2 colors should "flow" back and "seam up" slowly.
* When all the shells are decorated, bake them in the oven following instructions on pages 8–11.

### For the filling:

* Warm the cream on the stove over low heat until it boils.
* Remove the cream from the heat, pour it over the white chocolate, and mix until it is smooth and the chocolate is melted completely.
* Let the ganache cool in the refrigerator for about 1 hour.
* Pipe the macaron shells, add in 2–3 blueberries, and close up with another shell.

Makes 24 macaron shells of 1 1/2 inches (4cm)

Preparation : 30 minutes drying time

Cooking time : 12–15 minutes baking time + 30 minutes to prepare the filling

## Ingredients

### For the shells:

* 2 egg whites (80g)
* 1/3 cup (60g) superfine castor sugar

* 3/4 cup + 4 tsp (100g) powdered sugar
* 2/3 cup (60g) almond flour

* 1 tsp red food coloring powder
* 1 tsp yellow food coloring powder
* 1 tsp blue food coloring powder

### For the filling:

* 2.1 oz (60g) white chocolate (finely chopped)
* 1 tsp lemon juice
* 2.5 oz (70g) fresh or frozen berry mix (if using frozen fruit, thaw at room temperature)

## Methods

### For the shells:

* Please follow the instructions on pages 12–13.
* Bake at 300 °F (150 °C) for 12 minutes. Let the macaron shells cool down before removing them from the baking sheet.

### For the filling:

* Blend the berry mix and lemon juice. Pass the pulp through a sieve to remove any seeds and to obtain a smooth texture. Set aside in a small pot.
* Boil water in a medium pot. Melt the white chocolate in a heat-proof bowl set over a warm water bath.
* Stir until the chocolate has melted. Remove it from the heat.
* Gently warm up the blended berries over medium heat, stirring constantly.
* When warm enough, pour the berry mixture over the white chocolate. Then, stir well to combine.
* Leave to cool at room temperature before refrigerating for at least 2 hours for the ganache to harden.

Makes 24 macaron shells of 1 1/2 inches (4cm)
Preparation : 30 minutes drying time
Cooking time : 12–15 minutes baking time + 45 minutes to prepare the filling

## Ingredients

### For the shells:

* 1 egg white (40g)
* 2 1/2 tbsp superfine sugar

* 1/3 cup + 4 tsp (50g) powdered sugar
* 1/3 cup (30g) almond flour

* 1/4 tsp yellow food coloring powder

### For the filling:

* 1 bergamot orange (organic/untreated)

* 1.75 oz (50g) white chocolate (finely chopped)
* 2 tsp (10g) heavy cream (35% fat)
* 2 tsp (10g) bergamot juice
* zest from 1 bergamot

## Methods

### For the shells:

* Follow the basic macaron baking methods on pages 8–11.
* Bake at 300 °F (150 °C) for 12 minutes. Let the macaron shells cool down before removing them from the baking sheet.

### For the filling:

* Wash the fruit, and dry it well.
* Grate the zest, and set aside.
* Melt the chocolate over a water bath.
* Add the cream to a pot, and warm over medium heat until it boils.
* Pour it over the chocolate 3 times, mixing well after each addition. Mix the bergamot juice and the zest.
* Transfer into a small bowl and let cool in the refrigerator for 2 hours.

Makes 24 macaron shells of 1 1/2 inches (4cm)
Preparation : 30 minutes drying time
Cooking time : 12–15 minutes baking time + 45 minutes to prepare the filling

**Fraise :**
Strawberry & White Chocolate

## Ingredients

### For the shells:

* 1 egg white (40g)
* 2 1/2 tbsp (30g) superfine sugar

* 1/3 cup + 4 tsp (50g) powdered sugar
* 1/3 cup (30g) almond flour

* 1/4 tsp red food coloring powder
* metallic red food coloring (optional)

### For the filling:

* 1–2 strawberries~0.5 oz (10g) (cleaned and mashed)
* 1 fresh strawberry (diced)
* 1.75 oz (50g) white chocolate (finely chopped)
* 4 tsp (20g) heavy cream (35% fat)

## Methods

### For the shells:

* Follow the basic macaron baking methods on pages 8–11.
* Bake at 300 °F (150 °C) for 12 minutes. Let the macaron shells cool down before removing them from the baking sheet.
* Wet a paint brush, dip into the metallic food coloring, and brush over the baked shells.

### For the filling:

* Wash the strawberries, and dry them well. Purée 0.5 oz (10g) of the strawberries with a hand mixer.
* In a pot, add in strawberry and cream, and warm over medium heat.
* Melt the chocolate in a heat-proof bowl over a water bath.
* When the cream mixture is warm, pour it over the chocolate, and mix well.
* Add in the diced strawberry, stir, and transfer it into a small bowl. Let cool in the refrigerator for 2 hours.
* Fill the macarons 2–3 hours before serving to prevent soaking the shells because this filling is more moist than the standard ganache.

Makes 24 macaron shells of 1 1/2 inches (4cm)
Preparation : 30 minutes drying time
Cooking time : 12–15 minutes baking time + 45 minutes to prepare the filling

## Ingredients

### For the shells:

* 1 egg white (40g)
* 2 1/2 tbsp (30g) superfine sugar

* 1/3 cup + 4 tsp (50g) powdered sugar
* 1/3 cup (30g) almond flour

* 1/4 tsp red food coloring powder

### For the filling:

* 1 blood orange (organic/untreated)

* 1.75 oz (50g) white chocolate (finely chopped)
* 2 tsp (10g) heavy cream (35% fat)
* 2 tsp (10g) blood orange juice
* zest of 1 blood orange

## Methods

### For the shells:

* Follow the basic macaron baking methods on pages 8–11.
* Bake at 300 °F (150 °C) for 12 minutes. Let the macaron shells cool down before removing them from the baking sheet.

### For the filling:

* Wash the fruit, and dry them well.
* Grate the zest, and set aside.
* Melt the chocolate over a water bath.
* Add the cream, and warm over medium heat.  Stir well until it boils.
* Pour it over the chocolate  3 times, mixing well after each addition. Add the blood orange juice and the zest.
* Transfer into a small bowl and let cool in the refrigerator for 2 hours.

Orange Sanguine :
Blood Orange & White Chocolate

Makes 24 macaron shells of 1 1/2 inches (4cm)
Preparation : 30 minutes drying time
Cooking time : 12–15 minutes baking time + 45 minutes to prepare the filling

## Ingredients

### For the shells:

* 1 egg white (40g)
* 2 1/2 tbsp (30g) superfine sugar

* 1/3 cup + 4 tsp (50g) powdered sugar
* 1/3 cup (30g) almond flour

* 1/4 tsp yellow food coloring powder
* 1/4 tsp orange food coloring powder
* 1/4 tsp green food coloring powder

### For the filling:

* 3.5 oz (100g) mango (mashed and blended)
* 1 gelatin sheet
* 1/4 cup (50g) superfine sugar
* 1 egg
* 2 tsp (5g) cornstarch
* 5 tbsp (70g) butter (room temperature and cubed)

## Methods

### For the shells:

* Please follow the instructions on pages 12–13.
* Bake at 300 °F (150 °C) for 12 minutes. Let the macaron shells cool down before removing them from the baking sheet.

### For the filling:

* Peel the mango, chop, and blend it.
* Soak the gelatin sheet in cold water.
* Add the sugar, cornstarch, and egg to a pot. Whisk and heat over low heat until the mixture thickens. Keep whisking to prevent burning. Add in the mango purée.
* Bring the mixture to a boil. Squeeze out excess water from the gelatin, and add it into the mixture. Mix well until the gelatin is dissolved.
* Transfer the mixture into a mixing bowl, add the butter, and blend it until a smooth, creamy consistency is obtained.
* It is best to eat these macarons the same evening or the next day because the moisture from the cream might soften the shells.

Makes 24 macaron shells of 1 1/2 inches (4cm)

Preparation : 30 minutes drying time

Cooking time : 12–15 minutes baking time + 45 minutes to prepare the filling

## Ingredients

### For the shells:

* 1 egg white (40g)
* 2 1/2 tbsp (30g) superfine sugar

* 1/3 cup + 4 tsp (50g) powdered sugar
* 1/3 cup (30g) almond flour
* 1/2 tsp unsweetened cocoa powder

### For the filling:

* 2 oz (50g) apple (diced in cube)
* 1/2 tsp licorice powder
* 1 1/2 tbsp (20g) superfine sugar
* 2 tsp (10g) butter

## Methods

### For the shells:

* Follow the basic macaron baking methods on pages 8–11.
* Bake at 300 °F (150 °C) for 12 minutes. Let the macaron shells cool down before removing them from the baking sheet.

### For the filling:

* Add the butter, sugar, and diced apple to a nonstick pot. Heat until the sugar is melted and caramelizes the apple.
* Add in the licorice powder, and mix well.
* Remove from the heat once most of the moisture evaporates.
* Set aside to cool. Once cooled, place a small teaspon of caramelized apple on each shell.

Makes 24 macaron shells of 1 1/2 inches (4cm)
Preparation : 30 minutes drying time
Cooking time : 12–15 minutes baking time + 45 minutes to prepare the filling

## Ingredients

### For the shells:

* 1 egg white (40g)
* 2 1/2 tbsp (30g) superfine sugar

* 1/3 cup + 4 tsp (50g) powdered sugar
* 1/3 cup (30g) almond flour
* 1/2 tsp unsweetened cocoa powder

### For the filling:

* 1 lemon (zest removed and juiced)
* 1/4 cup (65g) sugar
* 1 egg
* 2/3 cup (145g) butter

* Half an egg white (20g)
* 1 1/2 tbsp (20g) sugar

## Methods

### For the shells:

* Follow the basic macaron baking methods on pages 8–11.
* Bake at 300 °F (150 °C) for 12 minutes. Let the macaron shells cool down before removing them from the baking sheet.

### For the filling:

* Add the egg and sugar to a medium mixing bowl, and mix well.
* Zest the lemon, and add it to a pot along with its juice. When the lemon juice is simmering, pour it over the egg mixture, and whisk at the same time. Mix well.
* Put the mixture back in the pot over medium heat, keep whisking until the mixture is thickened up, and keep whisking until some bubbles start to pop up.
* Remove from the heat. Add the butter, and blend it with a hand blender. Pour into a clean bowl, and place a cling wrap touching the cream. Put in the refrigerator until it is chilled (this can take a few hours).
* Before serving, whip up the egg white with the sugar to obtain a firm meringue. Pipe the lemon cream onto the shells, and add a small amount of meringue on top.
* It is best to eat these macarons the same evening or the next day because the moisture from the cream might soften the shells.

Makes 24 macaron shells of 1 1/2 inches (4cm)
Preparation : 30 minutes drying time
Cooking time : 12–15 minutes baking time + 30 minutes to prepare the filling

## Ingredients

### For the shells:

* 2 egg whites (80g)
* 1/3 cup (60g) superfine sugar

* 3/4 cup + 4 tsp (100g) powdered sugar
* 2/3 cup (60g) almond flour

* 1 tsp orange food coloring powder
* 1 tsp green food coloring powder

### For the filling:

* 2.8 oz (80g) white chocolate (finely chopped)
* 2 tbsp (30g) organic mandarin juice
* zest of 1 mandarin
* 2 tsp (10g) heavy cream

## Methods

### For the shells:

* Please follow the instructions on pages 12–13.
* Bake at 300 °F (150 °C) for 12 minutes. Let the macaron shells cool down before removing them from the baking sheet.

### For the filling:

* Warm up the mandarin juice and zest in a small pot.
* When it's warm enough, pour it over the white chocolate. Stir until the mixture is well combined.
* Warm up the cream, add it into the chocolate mixture, and mix well until a smooth consistency is obtained.
* Leave to cool at room temperature, and refrigerate for at least 2 hours for the ganache to harden.
* When it's ready, pipe it onto the macaron shells.

Makes 24 macaron shells of 1 1/2 inches (4cm)
Preparation : 30 minutes drying time
Cooking time : 12–15 minutes baking time + 45 minutes to prepare the filling

## Ingredients

### For the shells:

* 1 egg white (40g)
* 2 1/2 tbsp (30g) superfine sugar

* 1/3 cup + 4 tsp (50g) powdered sugar
* 1/4 cup (25g) almond flour
* 1 tsp (5g) dried coconut flakes (blend together)
* 1/4 tsp of white food coloring powder
* some marigold flower petal

### For the filling:

* 1/2 pomegranate (seeds only)
* juice of 1 kaffir lime
* 1 tbsp of coconut flakes
* 1.75 oz (50g) white chocolate (finely chopped)
* 1 1/2 tbsp (25g) heavy cream (35% fat)

## Methods

### For the shells:

* Follow the basic macaron baking methods on pages 8–11.
* Pipe the shells and sprinkle the marigold petals on top.
* Bake at 300 °F (150 °C) for 12 minutes. Let the macaron shells cool before removing them from the baking sheet.

### For the filling:

* Melt the white chocolate in a heat-proof bowl over a water bowl.
* Meanwhile, warm up the cream in another pot. When the chocolate is melted, pour it over the warm cream. Stir to mix well.
* Add the kaffir lime juice and coconut flakes. Stir until a smooth ganache is obtained.
* Fill one of the macaron shells with the chocolate ganache, place 3–4 pomegranate seeds over it, and place a tiny drop of chocolate on another shell, so that the shell sticks to the pomegranate seeds.
* It is best to eat these macarons the same evening or the next day because the moisture from the fresh pomegranate might soften the shells.

Makes 24 macaron shells of 1 1/2 inches (4cm)

Preparation : 30 minutes drying time

Cooking time : 12–15 minutes baking time + 45 minutes to prepare the filling

## Ingredients

### For the shells:

* 1 egg white (40g)
* 2 1/2 tbsp (30g) superfine sugar

* 1/3 cup + 4 tsp (50g) powdered sugar
* 1/3 cup (30g) almond flour
* 1/4 tsp orange powder food coloring

### For the filling:

* 4 tsp (20g) orange juice
* orange zest
* 1/4 tsp agar-agar powder

* 2 1/2 tbsp (40g) heavy cream (35% fat)
* 1.75 oz (50g) milk chocolate (chopped)

## Methods

### For the shells:

* Follow the basic macaron baking methods on pages 8–11.

### For the filling:

* Place the orange juice, zest, and agar-agar powder in a pot, and bring to boil for 1 minute. Pour onto small plates and refrigerate.
* Warm up the cream. Meanwhile, put the chocolate in a heat-proof bowl, and melt it over a water bath.
* When the cream is warm, pour it over chocolate. Mix well.
* Set the chocolate ganache aside to cool. Then, refrigerate until hardened.
* Pipe the ganache onto a shell, place a slice of the orange jelly in the middle, and close up with another shell.

Makes 24 macaron shells of 1 1/2 inches (4cm)
Preparation : 30 minutes drying time
Cooking time : 12–15 minutes baking time + 45 minutes to prepare the filling

## Ingredients

### For the shells:

* 1 egg white (40g)
* 2 1/2 tbsp (30g) superfine sugar

* 1/3 cup + 4 tsp (50g) powdered sugar
* 1/3 cup (30g) almond flour

* 1/4 tsp light green food coloring powder
* 1/4 tsp green food coloring powder

### For the filling:

* 1 lime

* 1.75 oz (50g) white chocolate (finely chopped)
* 1 tbsp (15g) heavy cream (35% fat)
* 2 tsp (10g) lime juice

## Methods

### For the shells:

* Follow the multi-colored macaron baking methods on pages 12–13. Separate the mixture into two, and add the light green food coloring powder to one bowl and the green food coloring powder to another.
* Fold and mix according to the instructions on pages 12–13. Fill the piping bag, and alternate the colors to get the marble effect when piped.
* Bake at 300 °F (150 °C) for 12 minutes. Let the macaron shells cool down before removing them from the baking sheet.

### For the filling:

* Wash the lime and dry it well.
* Grate the zest and set aside.
* Melt the chocolate over a water bath.
* Add the cream to a pot, and cook over medium heat. Stir well until it boils.
* Pour it over the chocolate and mix well. Add the lime juice and zest. Mix well.
* Transfer into a small bowl, and let cool to room temperature before refrigerating for 2 hours.

# thème & forme

{theme & shape}

Makes 24 macaron shells of 1 1/2 inches (4cm)
Preparation : 30 minutes drying time
Cooking time : 12–15 minutes baking time + 30 minutes to prepare the filling

## Ingredients

### For the shells:

* 1 egg white (40g)
* 2 1/2 tbsp (30g) superfine sugar

* 1/3 cup + 4 tsp (50g) powdered sugar
* 1/3 cup (30g) almond flour
* 1/4 tsp gold food coloring powder

* 1/2 tsp gold food coloring powder

### For the filling:

* 1 egg yolk
* 2 tbsp (25g) sugar
* 1 1/2 tsp (8g) water
* 1/4 cup (60g) butter (room temperature)
* 2 tbsp champagne or bubbly wine
* 2 tbsp (20g) popping sugar candy (unflavored)

## Methods

### For the shells:

* Follow the basic macaron baking methods on pages 8–11.
* Bake at 300 °F (150 °C) for 12 minutes. Let the macaron shells cool down before removing them from the baking sheet.
* Let the macaron shells cool down before removing them from the baking sheet.
* Using a sieve, sprinkle the gold food coloring over the baked shells.

### For the filling:

* Cut the butter into small cubes, and let it soften at room temperature.
* Mix the sugar and water in a small pot, and cook over medium heat. Start beating the egg yolk in a mixing bowl when the syrup temperature reaches 230 °F (110 °C) on a candy thermometer.
* Once the syrup temperature reaches 245 °F (118 °C), remove from the heat, and slowly pour it down the side of the bowl while beating the egg yolk using medium speed.
* Keep the mixer turning until the temperature of the mixture changes to lukewarm. Add in the butter one piece at a time, beat, and incorporate well after each addition.
* When all butter is fully incorporated, add in the popping candy, and mix lightly. Refrigerate for 10 minutes, and transfer into a piping bag. Fill the macaron shells.

Makes 24 macaron shells of 1 1/2 inches (4cm)
Preparation : 30 minutes drying time
Cooking time : 12–15 minutes baking time + 30 minutes to prepare the filling

## Ingredients

### For the shells:

* 1 egg white (40g)
* 2 1/2 tbsp (30g) superfine sugar

* 1/3 cup + 4 tsp (50g) powdered sugar
* 1/3 cup (30g) almond flour
* 1/2 tbsp red food coloring powder

### For the filling:

* 2 1/2 tbsp (40g) heavy cream (35% fat)
* 1.75 oz (50g) dark chocolate (finely chopped)
* 12 canned cherries (drained and halved)
* 1 tsp kirsch liqueur

## Methods

### For the shells:

* Follow the basic macaron baking method on pages 8–11.
* To make heart-shaped macarons, pipe half of the heart by simply pressing the piping bag and then releasing the pressure while dragging towards the pointed end. Repeat for the other half.
* Bake at 300 °F (150 °C) for 12 minutes. Let the macaron shells cool down before removing them from the baking sheet.

### For the filling:

* Put the dark chocolate in a heat-proof bowl, and melt it over a water bath. Remove from the heat when the chocolate is melted.
* Warm up the cream in a small pot, add in the kirsch liqueur, and bring to a boil. Pour 1/3 of it over the chocolate, and mix well. Repeat twice until a smooth ganache is obtained.
* To fill the macarons, pipe the ganache on one shell, top it up with a cherry, pipe a pea size over the cherry, and close up with another macaron shell.

Makes 24 macaron shells of 1 1/2 inches (4cm)
Preparation : 30 minutes drying time
Cooking time : 12–15 minutes baking time + 30 minutes to prepare the filling

## Ingredients

### For the shells:

* 1 egg white (40g)
* 2 1/2 tbsp (30g) superfine sugar

* 1/3 cup + 4 tsp (50g) powdered sugar
* 1/3 cup (30g) almond flour
* 1/4 tsp green food coloring powder

* pinch of green food coloring powder

### For the filling:

* 1 egg yolk
* 2 tbsp (30g) butter (cubed, room temperature)
* 2 tbsp (30g) salted butter (cubed, room temperature)
* 2 tbsp (25g) sugar
* 1 tbsp Manzana (apple liqueur)

## Methods

### For the shells:

* Follow the basic macaron baking methods on pages 8–11. Mix the dry and wet ingredients roughly, scoop out 1 tbsp, and put it in a separate bowl. Add in the dark green coloring powder, and mix until it is a bit runny.
* Fold the remaining ingredients, and pipe the macaron shells.
* Using a skewer or chopsticks, dip into the green mixture and slowly draw a clover on the shell.
* Bake at 300 °F (150 °C) for 12 minutes. Let the macaron shells cool down before removing them from the baking sheet.

### For the filling:

* Cut the butter into small cubes, and let it soften at room temperature.
* Mix the sugar and water in a small pot, and cook over medium heat.
* Start beating the egg yolk when the syrup temperature reaches 230 °F (110 °C) on a candy thermometer.
* Once the syrup temperature reaches 245 °F (118 °C), remove it from the heat, and slowly pour it down the side of the bowl while beating the egg yolk using medium speed.
* Keep the mixer turning until the mixture temperature has cooled down to lukewarm. Add in the butter one piece at a time, beat, and incorporate well after each addition. Lastly, add the Manzana, and beat until a smooth buttercream is obtained.
* Refrigerate for 10 minutes before transfer into a piping bag to fill the macaron shells.

Makes 10 bunny-shaped shells

Preparation : 30 minutes drying time

Cooking time : 12–15 minutes baking time + 30 minutes to prepare the filling

Note : For this recipe, you will need an extra piping bag and an extra No. 3 tip.

## Ingredients

### For the shells:

* 1 egg white (40g)
* 2 1/2 tbsp (30g) superfine sugar

* 1/3 cup + 4 tsp (50g) powdered sugar
* 1/3 cup (30g) almond flour

* food decorating pen in black & pink
* heart candy for decoration

### For the filling:

* 1/3 cup + 1 1/2 tbsp (100g) heavy cream (35% fat)
* 1 red fruit tea bag
* 1.75 oz (50g) dark chocolate (finely chopped)

## Methods

### For the shells:

* Follow the basic macaron baking method on pages 8–11.
* Put 1/4 of the mixture into a piping bag with a small tip. Set aside.
* Pour the other 3/4 of the mixture into another bag with a normal tip (No. 8).
* Pipe small ovals to make the body of the rabbit.
* Now take the other piping bag with the small tip prepared earlier, squeeze, and draw the ears on top of the oval, followed by the tail. Place the candy heart near the tail.
* Do this for half of the shells.
* Bake at 300 °F (150 °C) for 12 minutes. Let the macaron shells cool down before removing them from the baking sheet.
* When the macaron shells are cooled down, draw the bunny eyes and nose. Remove carefully because they are fragile.

### For the filling:

* Infuse the cream with the tea bag for 3 minutes. Meanwhile, put the chocolate in a heatproof bowl and melt it over a water bath.
* Squeeze out as much cream from the tea bag as possible. You will need 3 1/2 tablespoons of the infused cream to mix with the chocolate.
* Rewarm the cream, and pour 1/3 over the chocolate. Mix well, and repeat twice.
* Set the chocolate ganache aside to cool down. Then, refrigerate for 1–2 hours to harden.

Makes 24 macaron shells of 1 1/2 inches (4cm)
Preparation : 30 minutes drying time
Cooking time : 12–15 minutes baking time + 30 minutes to prepare the filling

## Ingredients

### For the shells:

* 1 egg white (40g)
* 2 1/2 tbsp (30g) sugar

* 1/3 cup + 4 tsp (50g) powdered sugar
* 1/3 cup (30g) almond flour

* sugar hearts for decoration

### For the filling:

* 3.5 oz (100g) red currants
* 1/2 tsp lemon juice
* 3 1/2 tbsp (40g) superfine sugar
* 1/4 tsp cornstarch
* 1/4 tsp agar-agar powder

## Methods

### For the shells:

* Follow the basic macaron baking methods on pages 8–11.
* Pipe the shells, and decorate half of them with sugar hearts.
* Bake at 300 °F (150 °C) for 12 minutes. Let the macaron shells cool down before removing them from the baking sheet.

### For the filling:

* Blend the red currants, cornstarch, and sugar.
* Pass through a sieve set over a small pot to remove any impurities from the juice.
* Add the lemon juice and agar-agar powder, stir, and boil the mixture for 3 minutes. Keep stirring to avoid burning.
* Remove from the heat, and transfer the mixture into a small bowl. Let it cool to room temperature before refrigerating.

Makes 24 macaron shells of 1 1/2 inches (4cm)

Preparation : 30 minutes drying time

Cooking time : 12–15 minutes baking time + 30 minutes to prepare the filling

Note: For this recipe, you will need 2 extra small piping bags and 1 extra mixing bowl

## Ingredients

### For the shells:

* 1 egg white (40g)
* 2 1/2 tbsp (30g) superfine sugar

* 1/3 cup + 4 tsp (50g) powdered sugar
* 1/3 cup (30g) almond flour

* 1/2 tsp black food coloring powder
* 1/2 tsp blue food coloring powder

### For the filling:

* 1.75 oz (50g) dark chocolate
* 1/3 cup + 1 1/2 tbsp (100g) heavy cream (35% fat)
* 1 vanilla bean
* 1 black tea bag

## Methods

### For the shells:

* Prepare 2 small piping bags for each color and a big piping bag with a No. 8 tip.
* Follow the multi-color macaron baking method on pages 12–13.
* Put the small piping bags into the big piping bag. Pipe the mixture in a small rectangular form by slowly dragging the bag sideways while pressing down slightly.
* Bake at 300 °F (150 °C) for 12 minutes. Let the macaron shells cool down before removing them from the baking sheet.

### For the filling:

* Halve the vanilla bean. Add the cream, tea bag, and vanilla bean to a pot, and warm up. Set aside for 10 minutes.
* Meanwhile, chop the dark chocolate, and melt it in a heat-proof bowl over a water bath.
* After 10 minutes squeeze out the rest of the cream from the bag, remove, and discard the tea bag. You will need 3 1/2 tablespoons of infused cream.
* Pour 1/3 of the warmed infused cream over the melted chocolate. Repeat this twice. Mix and incorporate well. Pour it into a small ramekin and cover with cling wrap touching the chocolate ganache.
* Set in refrigerator until the ganache hardens before piping. Refrigerate for 2 hours.

Makes 48 macaron shells of 1 1/2 inches (4 cm)
Preparation : 30 minutes drying time
Cooking time : 12–15 minutes baking time + 30 minutes to prepare the filling

## Ingredients

### For the shells:

* 2 egg whites (80g)
* 1/3 cup (60g) superfine sugar

* 3/4 cup + 4 tsp (100g) powdered
  sugar
* 2/3 cup (60g) almond flour

* food coloring powder: yellow, red,
  blue

### For the filling:

* 2 1/2 tbsp (40g) pineapple juice
  (unsweetened)
* 4 tsp (20g) cream (35% fat)
* 3.5 oz (100g) white chocolate
  (finely chopped)

*6–8 pieces of canned/ fresh pineapple
  (purée)

## Methods

### For the shells:

* You will need to bake two batches of shells. Each batch will have dif-
  ferent color combinations.
* Prepare three small piping bags and a big piping bag with tip No. 8
  on it.
* Follow the multi-color macaron baking methods on pages 12–13.
* Color the first batch yellow, orange (mix yellow+red), and red.
* Put the small piping bags into the big piping bag, and start piping.
* Bake at 300 °F (150 °C) for 12 minutes. Let the macaron shells cool
  down before removing them from the baking sheet.
* For the second batch, follow the same instruction above, but
  color the divided mixture green (blue+yellow), blue, and purple
  (blue+red).

### For the filling:

* Purée the pineapple, and pass it through a sieve. Set aside.
* Melt the white chocolate in a heat-proof bowl over a water bath.
* Warm up the pineapple juice and cream in a small pot. Add the
  purée, stir, and incorporate well.
* Remove from the heat, and pour 1/3 of the mixture over the melted
  chocolate. Repeat twice. Pour it into a bowl. Set aside to cool before
  refrigerating for 1–2 hours to harden.

Makes 8 macaron shells of 2 3/4 inches (7cm)

Preparation : 30 minutes drying time

Cooking time : 12–15 minutes baking time + 30 minutes to prepare the filling

Note: For this recipe, you will need 2 extra mixing bowls, a pair of chopsticks, and wooden skewers

## Ingredients

### For the shells:

* 1 egg white (40g)
* 2 1/2 tbsp (30g) superfine sugar

* 1/3 cup + 4 tsp (50g) powdered sugar
* 1/3 cup (30g) almond flour

* 1/4 tsp blue food coloring powder
* 1/4 tsp black food coloring powder
* pinch of red food coloring powder

### For the filling:

* 3 1/2 tbsp (50g) heavy cream (35% fat)
* 1.75 oz (50g) dark chocolate (finely chopped)
* 3 tbsp (30g) popping sugar (natural or flavored)

## Methods

### For the shells:

* Follow the basic macaron baking method on pages 8–11.
* Scoop 1 tbsp mixture out for each bowl. Add the red coloring powder to one bowl, and mix well.
* Add the blue coloring powder to the main mixing bowl, fold, and pipe eight circles measuring approximately 2 inches. To make the ears on four of them, pipe two small circles on each side. This will be the front.
* Dip the chopsticks into the white mixture, and dab lightly in the middle on the front side. Do the same for all four front sides.
* Dip another clean chopstick into the pink mixture, and slowly dab the side of the white circle and in the middle of each ear.
* Add the black coloring powder to the white mixture used earlier, mix well, and using the same method above, draw the eyes and the nose.
* Bake for 20 minutes following the basic methods on pages 8–11.

### For the filling:

* Melt the dark chocolate in a heat-proof bowl over a water bath.
* Warm up the cream, and pour 1/3 of it over the melted chocolate. Repeat twice. Let cool for 6 minutes before adding the popping sugar to prevent it from melting and popping.
* Mix lightly, and pour into a ramekin. Cover with cling wrap touching the ganache, and refrigerate for 1–2 hours.
* Pipe the chocolate ganache onto one macaron shell, place a wooden skewer on top, and close it up with another shell.

Makes 24 macaron shells of 1 1/2 inches (4cm)

Preparation : 30 minutes drying time

Cooking time : 12–15 minutes baking time + 30 minutes to prepare the filling

## Ingredients

### For the shells:

* 1 egg white (40g)
* 2 1/2 tbsp (30g) superfine sugar

* 1/3 cup + 4 tsp (50g) powdered sugar
* 1/3 cup (30g) almond flour

* 1/4 tsp black gel food coloring
* 1/4 tsp orange food coloring powder

### For the filling:

* 1.75 oz (50g) dark chocolate (finely chopped)
* 3 1/2 tbsp (50g) heavy cream (35%)
* dash of ground cinnamon
* 1 tbsp Grand Marnier®

## Methods

### For the shells:

* Follow the basic macaron baking method on pages 8–11.
* Mix the dry and wet ingredients roughly, scoop 1 tbsp out, and set aside in a small bowl. Add the orange coloring powder, and mix well until the mixture becomes a bit runny.
* Mix in the other coloring powders, and fold according to the methods on pages 8–11.
* Pipe the shells, and decorate them with the orange mixture. Dip a toothpick into the orange mixture, and lightly dot the piped shells.

### For the filling:

* Melt the chocolate in a heat-proof bowl over a water bath.
* Warm up the cream in a pot with a dash of cinnamon powder.
* Pour 1/3 of the warm cream over the melted chocolate, and mix well with a hand whisk. Repeat twice. Add in the Grand Marnier®, stir well, and pour into a ramekin. Cover with cling wrap touching the ganache. Refrigerate for 1 hour for the ganache to harden.

Makes 10 snowman macaron shells of 1 1/2 inches (4cm)

Preparation : 30 minutes drying time

Cooking time : 12–15 minutes baking time + 30 minutes to prepare the filling

## Ingredients

### For the shells:

* 1 egg white (40g)
* 2 1/2 tbsp (30g) superfine sugar

* 1/3 cup + 4 tsp (50g) powdered sugar
* 1/3 cup (30g) almond flour

* 1/4 tsp blue food coloring powder
* black icing pen

### For the filling:

* 3 1/2 tbsp (50g) heavy cream (35% fat)
* 1.75 oz (50g) dark chocolate (finely chopped)
* 1/4 tsp cinnamon
* 1/4 tsp ground anise
* 1/4 tsp anise (powder)
* 3 1/2 tbsp (50mL) red wine
* 1/4 tsp agar-agar powder

## Methods

### For the shells:

* Follow the basic macaron baking methods on pages 8–11.
* Scoop out 2 tbsp of the mixture into a separate bowl, and add in the blue coloring powder. Mix well and set aside.
* To make the snowman shape, pipe a circle of about 3/4 inch (2cm), and add a circle of about 1 1/2 inches (4cm) connected to the first circle. Repeat until the mixture is used up. Dip a chopstick in the blue mixture prepared earlier, and drag it between the two circles to make the scarf.
* Bake at 300 °F (150 °C) for 12 minutes. Let the macaron shells cool down before removing them from the baking sheet.

### For the filling:

* Mix the red wine and agar-agar powder in a small pot, and bring it to a boil for 2 minutes. Pour over a flat plate, and let it cool before refrigerating.
* Melt the dark chocolate in a heat-proof bowl over a water bath.
* In another pot, heat until just boiling the cream with cinnamon and anise powder. Remove from the heat, and infuse for 10 minutes.
* Rewarm the mixture, and pour it over the chocolate. Incorporate the mixture, and let it cool before refrigerating.
* Cut the jelly into small squares. Fill up one macaron shell with the chocolate ganache, top up with the jelly, and put a pea-size chocolate ganache on it. Close it up with another shell.

Makes 24 macaron shells of 1 1/2 inches (4cm)
Preparation : 30 minutes drying time
Cooking time : 12–15 minutes baking time + 1 hour to prepare the filling

## Ingredients

### For the shells:

* 1 egg white (40g)
* 2 1/2 tbsp (30g) superfine sugar

* 1/3 cup + 4 tsp (50g) powdered sugar
* 1/3 cup (30g) almond flour
* 1/2 tsp red food coloring powder

### For the filling:

* 2 1/2 tbsp (30g) superfine sugar
* 1 tbsp (16g) rose water

* 1 egg yolk
* 1/4 cup (60g) butter (room temperature, cubed)
* dried rose petals (optional)

## Methods

### For the shells:

* Follow the basic macaron baking methods on pages 8–11.
* Bake at 300 °F (150 °C) for 12 minutes. Let the macaron shells cool down before removing them from the baking sheet.

### For the filling:

* Warm the sugar and rose water in a pot over medium heat. Start beating the egg yolk when the temperature of the syrup reaches 237 °F (114 °C).
* When the temperature reaches 245 °F (118 °C), remove the syrup from the heat, and slowly pour it down the side of the bowl while beating the egg yolk using medium speed. Keep the mixer turning until the mixture has cooled down slightly. Add the butter one piece at a time, beat, and incorporate well after each addition.
* Lastly, add in the dried rose petals (if using). Mix well until a smooth buttercream is obtained.
* Fill half the macaron shells with the buttercream, and place another shell on top.

Makes 18 wombat-shaped shells of 1 1/2 inches (4cm)

Preparation : 30 minutes drying time

Cooking time : 12–15 minutes baking time + 30 minutes to prepare the filling

Note : For this recipe, you will need an extra piping bag and an extra No. 3 tip.

## Ingredients

### For the shells:

* 1 egg white (40g)
* 2 1/2 tbsp (30g) superfine sugar

* 1/3 cup + 4 tsp (50g) powdered sugar
* 1/3 cup (30g) almond flour
* 1/2 tbsp cocoa powder

* black and pink icing pens

### For the filling:

* 2 1/2 tbsp (40g) heavy cream (35% fat)
* 1.75 oz (50g) milk chocolate (finely chopped)
* 1 1/2 tbsp (9g) ground hazelnuts
* 2 tsp (10g) butter (cubed, room temperature)

## Methods

### For the shells:

* Follow the basic macaron baking method on pages 8–11.
* Put 1/4 of the mixture into the piping bag with the small tip. Set aside.
* Pour the other 3/4 of the mixture into the other bag with the No. 8 tip.
* Pipe out round shapes. Once finished, using the other piping bag with small tip prepared earlier, slowly squeeze and draw the ears on top.
* Do this on half of the shells.
* Bake at 300 °F (150 °C) for 12 minutes. Let the macaron shells cool down before removing them from the baking sheet.
* When the shells are cooled down, draw the eyes and nose. Remove carefully because they are fragile.

### For the filling:

* Warm up the cream. Meanwhile, melt the chocolate in a heat-proof bowl over a water bath.
* When the cream is warm, pour it over the chocolate, mix well, and add the ground hazelnuts and butter. Blend until a smooth ganache is obtained.
* Set the chocolate ganache aside to cool. Refrigerate until the texture is slightly hardened.

Makes 20 apple-shaped shells of 1 1/2 inches (4cm)

Preparation : 30 minutes drying time

Cooking time : 12–15 minutes baking time + 30 minutes to prepare the filling

Note : For this recipe, you will need an extra piping bag and an extra No. 3 tip.

## Ingredients

### For the shells:

* 1 egg white (40g)
* 2 1/2 tbsp (30g) superfine sugar

* 1/3 cup + 4 tsp (50g) powdered sugar
* 1/3 cup (30g) almond flour (blend together)
* 1/2 tsp red food coloring paste
* 1/4 tsp yellow food coloring powder

### For the filling:

* 2 tbsp (30g) heavy cream (35% fat)
* 1.75 oz (50g) Valrhona white chocolate (finely chopped)
* 1 1/2 tsp (10g) Pomme d'Amour syrup

## Methods

### For the shells:

* Follow the multi-colored macaron baking instructions on pages 12–13.
* Add the blended dry ingredients to the stiff egg white, and mix them up roughly. Scoop half of the mixture into an extra bowl, add in the yellow food coloring powder, and fold it well until it flows like a thick ribbon when lifted. In the main bowl add in red coloring and start folding.
* Keep folding until you get a uniform and shiny mixture, flowing down and forming a thick ribbon.
* Put a piece of parchment paper over a baking tray, and fill the piping bag by alternating the red and yellow mixture - one scoop yellow, one scoop red.
* Pipe the mixture by making two slight diagonal lines to create the form of an apple.
* Bake at 300 °F (150 °C) for 12 minutes. Let the macaron shells cool down before removing them from the baking sheet.

### For the filling:

* Warm up the cream and syrup in a pot. Meanwhile, melt the chocolate in a heat-proof bowl over a water bath.
* When the mixture is warm, pour it over the chocolate, mixing well until a smooth ganache is obtained.
* Set the chocolate ganache aside to cool. Then, refrigerate it until the texture is slightly hardened.

Makes 20 banana-shaped shells of 2 inches (5cm) by 3/4 inch (2cm)
Preparation : 30 minutes drying time
Cooking time : 12–15 minutes baking time + 30 minutes to prepare the filling
Note : For this recipe, you will need an extra piping bag and an extra No. 3 tip.

## Ingredients

### For the shells:

* 1 egg white (40g)
* 2 1/2 tbsp (30g) superfine sugar

* 1/3 cup + 4 tsp (50g) powdered sugar
* 1/3 cup (30g) almond flour
* 1/4 tsp yellow food coloring powder

* black food coloring pen

### For the filling:

* 3 1/2 tbsp (50g) heavy cream (35% fat)
* 1.75 oz (50g) dark chocolate (finely chopped)
* 1 1/2 tbsp (10g) banana (mashed)
* 2 tsp (10g) butter

## Methods

### For the shells:

* Follow the basic macaron instructions on pages 8–11.
* Fill the extra piping bag, reserving 2 tbsp of the mixture.
* Fill the other piping bag with the rest of the mixture, and pipe it into moon shapes. When the mixture is used up, using the other bag, pipe the end of the banana.
* Bake at 300 °F (150 °C) for 12 minutes. Let the macaron shells cool down before removing them from the baking sheet.
* When the shells are baked, using the food coloring pen, paint the end of each shell.

### For the filling:

* Warm up the cream in a pot. Meanwhile, melt the chocolate in a heat-proof bowl over a water bath.
* When the cream is warm, pour it over the chocolate, mixing well until a smooth ganache is obtained.
* Add the banana and butter, and blend everything with a hand mixer.
* Cover with cling wrap over the ganache, and keep it in the refrigerator until the ganache is slightly hardened.

Makes 10 kitty-shaped shells of 1 inch (3cm)
Preparation : 30 minutes drying time
Cooking time : 12–15 minutes baking time + 30 minutes to prepare the filling
Note : For this recipe, you will need an extra piping bag and an extra No. 3 tip.

## Ingredients

### For the shells:

* 1 egg white (40g)
* 2 1/2 tbsp (30g) superfine sugar

* 1/3 cup + 4 tsp (50g) powdered sugar
* 1/3 cup (30g) almond flour

* black and pink food decorating pens
* orange and black food coloring powders

### For the filling:

* candied orange peel (chopped)
* 1.75 oz (50g) dark chocolate (finely chopped)
* 3 1/2 tbsp (50g) heavy cream (35% fat)

## Methods

### For the shells:

* Follow the basic macaron baking method on pages 8–11. Mix the dry ingredients and stiffened egg white roughly, and scoop out 2 tbsp of the mixture into a small bowl.
* Add the food coloring powder to the main bowl, fold, and mix following the instructions on pages 8–11.
* Put 1/4 of the mixture into the piping bag with the small tip. Set aside.
* Pour the other 3/4 of the mixture into the bag with the No. 8 tip.
* Pipe out round shapes. Once finished, using the other piping bag with the small tip prepared earlier, slowly squeeze and draw the ears on top.
* Dip a stick into the white mixture, and dab it into the piped shell to create the white circle. Do this on half the shells.
* Bake at 300 °F (150 °C) for 12 minutes. Let the macaron shells cool down before removing them from the baking sheet.
* When the macaron shells are cooled down, draw the eyes, nose, and moustache. Remove carefully because they are fragile.

### For the filling:

* Melt the chocolate in a heat-proof bowl over a water bath.
* Meanwhile, warm up the cream in another pot.
* When the chocolate is melted, pour the warm cream over it, and stir to mix well. Set aside to let the ganache cool down.
* Fill one macaron shell with the chocolate ganache, place a piece of candied orange in the middle, and close up with another shell.

Makes 20 peanut-shaped shells of 2 inches (5cm)
Preparation : 30 minutes drying time
Cooking time : 12–15 minutes baking time + 30 minutes to prepare the filling

## Ingredients

### For the shells:

* 1 egg white (40g)
* 2 1/2 tbsp (30g) superfine sugar

* 1/3 cup + 4 tsp (50g) powdered sugar
* 1/3 cup (30g) almond flour
* 1/2 tsp unsweetened cocoa

* black food coloring pen

### For the filling:

* 3.5 oz (100g) roasted peanuts
* 1/4 tsp kosher salt
* 1/2 tsp honey
* 1/2 tbsp (70g) peanut oil

## Methods

### For the shells:

* Follow the basic macaron baking instructions on pages 8–11.
* Fill the piping bag with the rest of the mixture, then pipe the batter into a small circle of about 3/4 inch (2cm) and connected larger circle of about 1 1/2 inches (4cm) at the bottom.
* Bake at 300 °F (150 °C) for 12 minutes. Let the macaron shells cool down before removing them from the baking sheet.
* When the shells are baked, paint them with the food coloring pen.

### For the filling:

* Place the peanuts, salt, and honey into the bowl of a food processor.
* Process for 1 minute. Scrape down the sides of the bowl.
* Place the lid back on, and continue to process while slowly drizzling in the oil, and process until the mixture is smooth.

Makes 10 doughnut-shaped shells of 3 inches (8cm)
Preparation : 30 minutes drying time
Cooking time : 12–15 minutes baking time + 30 minutes to prepare the filling

## Ingredients

### For the shells:

* 1 egg white (40g)
* 2 1/2 tbsp (30g) superfine sugar

* 1/3 cup + 4 tsp (50g) powdered sugar
* 1/3 cup (30g) almond flour
* 1/2 tsp unsweetened cocoa

* roasted almond flakes

### For the filling:

Praline:
* 1.25 oz (35g) blanched whole almonds
* 1.25 oz (35g) blanched hazelnuts
* 1/3 cup (75g) granulated sugar

Crème pâtissière:
* 2 egg yolks
* 1/4 cup (55g) superfine sugar
* 1 1/2 tbsp (13g) cornstarch
* 2/3 cup (160mL) milk
* 1/3 cup + 1 tbsp (93mL) heavy cream, whisked into soft peaks

## Methods

### For the shells:

* Draw ten 3-inch diameter circles on the parchment paper, and flip it over to use the tracing as a guide.
* Follow the basic macaron baking instructions on pages 8–11.
* Pipe the mixture following the trace to make doughnuts.
* Sprinkle the roasted almond flakes over the piped shells.
* Bake according to the instruction on pages 8–11, but leave for 2–3 minutes longer in the oven because the size of the shells is larger.

### For the filling:

* For the praline, lightly oil a baking sheet. Put the almonds, hazelnuts, and sugar into a large heavy pan over a low heat. Stir occasionally until the sugar has melted and is beginning to caramelize. Continue to cook until the nuts are well-coated and the melted sugar is a deep golden brown.
* Pour on the oiled sheet, and leave until cold. Break up, put in a food processor, and process to a powder.
* For the crème pâtissière, place egg yolks and a third of the sugar in a bowl. Whisk until pale. Sift in the cornstarch, and mix. Put the milk and the remaining sugar in a pot, and bring to a boil.
* As soon as it bubbles, slowly pour it into the egg mixture, whisking continuously. Then, return to the pan, and cook over low heat while stirring. It will begin to thicken. Continue to stir and heat. When the mixture bubbles, the cream is ready.
* Pour the cream over a baking tray, and cover with a sheet of cling wrap. Freeze for 30 minutes.
* When cold, place in a bowl, and whisk until soft and creamy. Whisk in the praline, and fold in the whipped cream.

# cocktails

# {cocktails}

Makes 24 macaron shells of 1 1/2 inches (4cm)

Preparation : 30 minutes drying time

Cooking time : 12–15 minutes baking time + 25 minutes to prepare the filling

* Note: For this recipe, you will need 2 piping bags, a small No. 3 tip, and a normal No. 8 tip.

## Ingredients

### For the shells:

* 1 egg white (40g)
* 2 1/2 tbsp (30g) superfine sugar

* 1/3 cup + 4 tsp (50g) powdered sugar
* 1/3 cup (30g) almond flour

* 1/4 tsp yellow food coloring powder
* 1/4 tsp green food coloring powder

### For the filling:

* 2 tsp (10g) coconut milk
* 1 tbsp (15g) pineapple juice
* 1.75 oz (50g) white chocolate
* 1–2 drops rum flavoring

## Methods

### For the shells:

* Blend the almond flour and powdered sugar.
* Follow the basic macaron baking method on pages 8–11.
* Mix the dry and wet ingredients roughly, scoop up 2 tbsp of the mixture, and put in a separate bowl. Add the green food coloring powder, and fold the mixture. Pour it into the piping bag with the No. 3 tip.
* Add the yellow food coloring powder to the other bowl, fold, and pour into the piping bag with the No. 8 tip. Pipe the entire yellow mixture. Then, squeeze a small amount of the green mixture in the middle of the piped shells to make a spot.
* Bake at 300 °F (150 °C) for 12 minutes. Let the macaron shells cool down before removing them from the baking sheet.

### For the filling:

* Chop the white chocolate into small pieces, and set aside.
* In a small pot, mix the coconut milk and pineapple juice together, and warm over medium heat.
* Remove from heat, then pour it over the white chocolate. Stir and incorporate well.
* Add the rum flavoring, and mix well.
* Set aside to cool to room temperature, then refrigerate for 1–2 hours until the chocolate ganache is slightly hardened before filling the macarons.

Makes 24 macaron shells of 1 1/2 inches (4cm)

Preparation : 30 minutes drying time

Cooking time : 12–15 minutes baking time + 45 minutes to prepare the filling

## Ingredients

### For the shells:

* 1 egg white (40g)
* 2 1/2 tbsp (30g) superfine sugar

* 1/3 cup + 4 tsp (50g) powdered sugar
* 1/3 cup (30g) almond flour

* purple liquid food coloring
* 3 tsp (15g) granulated sugar

### For the filling:

Salted Butter Caramel:
* 3 1/2 tbsp (50g) heavy cream (35% fat)
* 1/3 cup (60g) superfine sugar
* 2 tsp (10g) salted butter (cubed, room temperature)

Baileys Buttercream:
* 2 1/2 tbsp (35g) butter
* 1 1/2 tbsp (20g) salted butter (cubed, room temperature)
* 2 tsp (10g) Baileys Irish Cream

## Methods

### For the shells:

* Mix the food coloring with the sugar to obtain colored sugar.
* Refer to the basic macaron making method on pages 8–11.
* When the shells are piped, sprinkle the colored sugar over them before baking.
* Bake at 300 °F (150 °C) for 12 minutes. Let the macaron shells cool down before removing them from the baking sheet.

### For the filling:

Salted Butter Caramel:
* Put the sugar into a clean pot, and cook over high heat. Stir it continuously with a hand whisk. The sugar will start to melt and brown slowly. Continue stirring to prevent burning.
* When the sugar turns into a syrup and caramelizes, turn down the heat to medium, add the salted butter, and keep stirring until everything is well incorporated.
* Be very careful! Because the caramel is very hot, the cold cream might splatter. Pour 1/3 of the cream into the caramel while stirring. Repeat until the cream is used up.
* Remove from the heat, pour it into a bowl, and set aside to cool.

Baileys Buttercream:
* Warm up the Baileys in a clean pot, and pour it over the butter.
* With an electric beater, whip up the mixture until all the butter is melted and incorporated with the Baileys.
* Add in the cooled salted butter caramel prepared earlier in the bowl, and whip until a smooth and thick buttercream is obtained.

Makes 24 macaron shells of 1 1/2 inches (4cm)
Preparation : 30 minutes drying time
Cooking time : 12–15 minutes baking time + 30 minutes to prepare the filling

## Ingredients

### For the shells:

* 1 egg white (40g)
* 2 1/2 tbsp (30g) superfine sugar

* 1/3 cup + 4 tsp (50g) powdered sugar
* 1/3 cup (30g) almond flour

### For the filling:

* 1/4 tsp brown powdered food coloring
* 4 tsp (20g) heavy cream (35%)
* 1.75 oz (50g) white chocolate
* 2 tsp (10g) white rum
* 1 tbsp (10g) raisins

## Methods

### For the shells:

* Follow the basic macaron baking methods on pages 8–11.
* After folding the dry and wet ingredients, scoop out 1 tbsp of the mixture into a small bowl before pouring them into the piping bag.
* Add brown coloring to the scooped out mixture, and mix well.
* Pipe the macaron shells. Dip a chopstick into the brown mixture, and drag it slowly over the piped shells.
* To make the swirl pattern, use a toothpick, stick lightly into the piped shell, and drag it from side to side.
* Bake at 300 °F (150 °C) for 12 minutes. Let the macaron shells cool before removing them from the baking sheet.

### For the filling:

* Soak the raisins in the rum for 2 hours.
* Chop up the white chocolate and melt it in a heat-proof bowl over a water bath.
* In a small pot, heat up the cream with the rum and raisins.
* Pour it over the melted chocolate 3 times, stirring and mixing well until everything is well incorporated.
* Transfer into a small bowl with the cling wrap touching the ganache, and refrigerate for 2 hours.
* Pipe the chocolate ganache onto the macaron shells.

Makes 24 macaron shells of 1 1/2 inches (4cm)
Preparation : 30 minutes drying time
Cooking time : 12–15 minutes baking time + 30 minutes to prepare the filling

## Ingredients

### For the shells:

* 1 egg white (40g)
* 2 1/2 tbsp (30g) superfine sugar

* 1/3 cup + 4 tsp (50g) powdered sugar
* 1/3 cup (30g) almond flour
* 1/2 tsp purple food coloring powder

* 1/4 tsp metallic silver food coloring powder
* 2 tbsp (25g) superfine sugar

### For the filling:

* 2.1 oz (60g) white chocolate (finely chopped)
* 2.1 oz (60g) black currants
* 1 tsp lemon juice
* 2 tsp (10g) heavy cream (35% fat)
* 1 tbsp crème de cassis (see glossary pages 198–199)

## Methods

### For the shells:

* To make the metallic-colored sugar, mix the 2 tbsp sugar with the food coloring powder in a small bowl. Wet a spoon lightly, then toss the sugar and the coloring together. Spread over a piece of parchment paper, and let it air-dry.
* Bake at 300 °F (150 °C) for 12 minutes. Let the macaron shells cool down before removing them from the baking sheet.
* Sprinkle the colored sugar over the shells before removing them from the baking sheet.

### For the filling:

* Mix the black currants and lemon juice with an immersion mixer.
* Press through a sieve to filter the pulp and seeds in order to obtain a smooth fruit purée. You should get roughly 3/4 oz (20–25g) of purée.
* Melt the chocolate in a heat-proof bowl over a water bath.
* Meanwhile, warm the black currant purée and heavy cream in a small pot over medium heat.
* Pour it over the melted chocolate, and mix well with a hand whisk until a smooth ganache is obtained.
* Lastly, add in the crème de cassis, and mix well.

Makes 24 macaron shells of 1 1/2 inches (4cm)

Preparation : 30 minutes drying time

Cooking time : 12–15 minutes baking time + 30 minutes to prepare the filling

## Ingredients

### For the shells:

* 1 egg white (40g)
* 2 1/2 tbsp (30g) superfine sugar

* 1/3 cup + 4 tsp (50g) powdered sugar
* 1/3 cup (30g) almond flour

* 1/2 tsp red food coloring powder

### For the filling:

* 1.75 oz (50g) dark chocolate (finely chopped)
* 3 1/2 tbsp (50g) heavy cream (35% fat)
* 1 tbsp raspberry vodka

## Methods

### For the shells:

* Follow the basic macaron methods on pages 8–11.
* Mix the dry ingredients with the stiff-peaked meringue. Fold until roughly combined. Scoop out 2 tbsp of the mixture into a smaller bowl, and mix well until watery.
* Add the red food coloring powder into the mixture in the main bowl.
* Pipe the shells. Once the red mixture is used up, dip a toothpick into the white mixture, and draw on the piped shells.
* Bake at 300 °F (150 °C) for 12 minutes. Let the macaron shells cool down before removing them from the baking sheet.

### For the filling:

* Melt the chocolate in a heat-proof bowl over a water bath.
* Meanwhile, heat the cream and raspberry vodka in a small pot over medium heat.
* Pour it over the melted chocolate, and mix well until a smooth ganache is obtained.
* Leave it to cool, and refrigerate until set.

Makes 24 macaron shells of 1 1/2 inches (4cm)
Preparation : 30 minutes drying time
Cooking time : 12–15 minutes baking time + 30 minutes to prepare the filling

## Ingredients

### For the shells:

* 1 egg white (40g)
* 2 1/2 tbsp (30g) superfine sugar

* 1/3 cup + 4 tsp (50g) powdered sugar
* 1/3 cup (30g) almond flour
* 1/2 tsp green food coloring powder

* walnuts (crushed)

### For the filling:

* 1.75 oz (50g) white chocolate (finely chopped)
* 4 tsp (20g) heavy cream (35% fat)
* 1 tsp Calvados liqueur
* candied ginger (diced)

## Methods

### For the shells:

* Follow the basic macaron methods on pages 8–11.
* Pipe the shells. Once the red mixture is used up, sprinkle the crushed walnut over the shells.
* Bake at 300 °F (150 °C) for 12 minutes. Let the macaron shells cool down before removing them from the baking sheet.

### For the filling:

* Melt the chocolate in a heat-proof bowl over a water bath.
* Meanwhile, heat the cream and Calvados in a small pot over medium heat.
* Pour it over the melted chocolate, and mix well until a smooth ganache is obtained.
* Leave it to cool, and refrigerate until set.
* Pipe the shells, place a cube of confit ginger in the middle, and close up with another shell.

Makes 24 macaron shells of 1 1/2 inches (4cm)

Preparation : 30 minutes drying time

Cooking time : 12–15 minutes baking time + 30 minutes to prepare the filling

## Ingredients

### For the shells:

* 1 egg white (40g)
* 2 1/2 tbsp (30g) superfine sugar

* 1/3 cup + 4 tsp (50g) powdered sugar
* 1/3 cup (30g) almond flour
* 1/2 tsp unsweetened cocoa powder

* 0.7 oz (20g) dark chocolate
* chocolate flakes

### For the filling:

* 2 1/2 tsp (10g) drunken cherries
* 1 1/2 tbsp (20g) kirsch liqueur
* 1/4 tsp agar-agar powder
* 1.75 oz (50g) dark chocolate (finely chopped)
* 3 1/2 tbsp (50g) heavy cream (35% fat)

## Methods

### For the shells:

* Follow the basic macaron methods on pages 8–11.
* Bake at 300 °F (150 °C) for 12 minutes. Let the macaron shells cool down before removing them from the baking sheet.
* Melt the dark chocolate over a water bath, and place the chocolate flakes in a small bowl.
* Dip the cool macarons into the melted chocolate and then into the chocolate flakes. Place on a parchment-lined baking sheet.
* Refrigerate until the chocolate is set.

### For the filling:

* To make the jelly, mince the drunken cherries and put them in a small pot. Add the kirsch liqueur and agar-agar powder. Stir and bring to a boil. Boil for 1 minute.
* Pour onto a small plate, and let harden in the refrigerator.
* Melt the chocolate in a heat-proof bowl over a water bath.
* Meanwhile, warm the heavy cream over medium heat.
* Pour it over the melted chocolate, and mix well until a smooth ganache is obtained.
* Leave it to cool at room temperature, and refrigerate until set.
* When the jelly is set, cut it up into small rectangles.
* Pipe the shells, place a slice of jelly in the middle of each shell, add a pea-size piece of ganache on the other shell, and close it up.

Makes 24 macaron shells of 1 1/2 inches (4cm)
Preparation : 30 minutes drying time
Cooking time : 12–15 minutes baking time + 30 minutes to prepare the filling

## Ingredients

### For the shells:

* 1 egg white (40g)
* 2 1/2 tbsp (30g) superfine sugar

* 1/3 cup + 4 tsp (50g) powdered sugar
* 1/3 cup (30g) almond flour
* 1/2 tbsp unsweetened cocoa powder

* pasteurized egg white
* colored sugar

### For the filling:

* 1/4 tsp (1g) gelatin powder
* 1 tsp (5g) water

* 1 egg yolk
* 2 1/2 tsp (10g) sugar
* 2 tbsp (15g) cornstarch

* 1/3 cup (85g) milk
* 1/3 cup (85g) Baileys Irish Cream

* 1/3 cup (60g) superfine sugar

* 6 1/2 tbsp (90g) butter

## Methods

### For the shells:

* Follow the basic macaron methods on pages 8–11.
* Bake at 300 °F (150 °C) for 12 minutes. Let the macaron shells cool down before removing them from the baking sheet.
* Once the shells are baked, brush them lightly with egg white, and dip into the colored sugar.

### For the filling:

* Mix the gelatin and water in a small bowl, and place in the refrigerator.
*Whisk the egg yolk and sugar in a mixing bowl. Add the cornstarch, and mix until smooth. Set aside.
* Place the milk and Baileys in a pot, and bring to a boil.
* Meanwhile, place 1/3 cup (60g) superfine sugar in a medium copper pot over medium heat. Stir constantly with a whisk to avoid burning until all the sugar is melted and a golden brown caramel forms.
* Remove the pot from the heat. Pour the milk mixture over the caramel, and keep stirring until smooth. Be careful because the caramel might spurt out when mixing.
* Put the pot back over medium heat, and bring mixture to a boil. When the caramel is boiled up, pour half of the mixture into the egg yolk mixture prepared earlier, and stir. Whisk well, and pour back into the pot.
* Keep stirring and whisking until the mixture thickens. It is ready when bubbles pop up from the bottom.
* Transfer the caramel to a clean bowl, add in the butter, and blend it. Leave to cool in the refrigerator until set.

Makes 24 macaron shells of 1 1/2 inches (4cm)

Preparation : 30 minutes drying time

Cooking time : 12–15 minutes baking time + 30 minutes to prepare the filling

## Ingredients

### For the shells:

* 1 egg white (40g)
* 2 1/2 tbsp (30g) superfine sugar

* 1/3 cup + 4 tsp (50g) powdered sugar
* 1/3 cup (30g) almond flour
* 1/2 tsp unsweetened cocoa powder

* gold metallic food coloring powder

### For the filling:

* 1.75 oz (50g) dark chocolate (finely chopped)
* 2 tbsp (30g) heavy cream (35% fat)
* 4 tsp (20g) whiskey

## Methods

### For the shells:

* Follow the basic macaron methods on pages 8–11.
* Bake at 300 °F (150 °C) for 12 minutes. Let the macaron shells cool down before removing them from the baking sheet.
* Once the shells are baked, moisten a small paint brush, dip it into the gold metallic food coloring powder, and brush it over the shells.

### For the filling:

* Melt the chocolate in a heat-proof bowl over a water bath.
* Meanwhile, warm the heavy cream and whiskey over medium heat.
* Pour it over the melted chocolate, and mix well until a smooth ganache is obtained.
* Leave it to cool at room temperature, and refrigerate until set.

Makes 24 macaron shells of 1 1/2 inches (4cm)
Preparation : 30 minutes drying time
Cooking time : 12–15 minutes baking time + 30 minutes to prepare the filling

## Ingredients

### For the shells:

* 1 egg white (40g)
* 2 1/2 tbsp (30g) superfine sugar

* 1/3 cup + 4 tsp (50g) powdered sugar
* 1/3 cup (30g) almond flour
* 1/2 tbsp green food coloring powder

* candied mint leaves (optional)

### For the filling:

* 1.75 oz (50g) white chocolate (finely chopped)
* 4 tsp (20g) heavy cream (35% fat)
* 1 tsp (5g) crème de menthe liqueur

## Methods

### For the shells:

* Follow the basic macaron baking methods on pages 8–11.
* If using candied mint leaves, sprinkle them over the shells before putting them in the over.
* Bake at 300 °F (150 °C) for 12 minutes. Let the macaron shells cool down before removing them from the baking sheet.

### For the filling:

* Melt the chocolate in a heat-proof bowl over a water bath.
* Meanwhile, warm the cream and crème de menthe over medium heat.
* Pour it over the melted chocolate, and mix well until a smooth ganache is obtained.
* Leave it to cool at room temperature, and refrigerate until set.

audacieux

{adventurous}

Makes 24 macaron shells of 1 1/2 inches (4cm)

Preparation : 30 minutes drying time

Cooking time : 12–15 minutes baking time + 25 minutes to prepare the filling

* Note: For this recipe, you will need 2 piping bags, a small No. 3 tip, and a normal No. 8 tip.

## Ingredients

### For the shells:

* 1 egg white (40g)
* 2 1/2 tbsp (30g) superfine sugar

* 1/3 cup + 4 tsp (50g) powdered sugar
* 1/3 cup (30g) almond flour

* 1/2 tsp black food coloring paste
* 1/4 tsp red food coloring powder

### For the filling:

* 1.75 oz (50g) dark chocolate
* 1/4 cup (60g) heavy cream (35% fat)
* 1/2 vanilla bean (seeds removed)
* 1/2 tsp Espelette chili flakes (see glossary pages 198–199)

* 2 drops Tabasco sauce

## Methods

### For the shells:

* Blend the almond flour and powdered sugar in a blender.
* Follow the basic macaron methods on pages 8–11.
* Mix the dry and wet ingredients roughly, scoop up 2 tbsp of the mixture, and put it in a separate bowl. Add the red food coloring powder, and fold the mixture. Pour in the piping bag with the No. 3 tip.
* Add the black food coloring paste to the other bowl, fold, and pour into the piping bag with the No. 8 tip. Pipe the mixture. Then, squeeze a small amount of the red mixture over the piped shells to make a red line.
* Bake at 300 °F (150 °C) for 12 minutes. Let the macaron shells cool down before removing them from the baking sheet.

### For the filling:

* In a small pan, roast the vanilla bean until fragrant.
* Add the cream, vanilla bean seeds, and Espelette chili flakes. Set aside to infuse for 5 minutes.
* Meanwhile, chop the dark chocolate into small pieces, and melt it in a water bath over medium heat. Remove from heat once the chocolate has melted.
* Over medium heat, bring the infused mixture to a boil. Remove from heat, and pour over the chocolate.
* Stir and incorporate well, and add in 2 drops of Tabasco sauce before transferring the ganache to small ramekins.
* Set aside at room temperature to cool down, then cover with cling wrap before refrigerating for 1–2 hours.

Makes 24 macaron shells of 1 1/2 inches (4cm)
Preparation : 30 minutes drying time
Cooking time : 12–15 minutes baking time + 30 minutes to prepare the filling

## Ingredients

### For the shells:

* 1 egg white (40g)
* 2 1/2 tbsp (30g) superfine sugar

* 1/3 cup + 4 tsp (50g) powdered sugar
* 1/3 cup (30g) almond flour

* 1/4 tsp red food coloring powder

### For the filling:

* 2 tbsp (30g) heavy cream (35% fat)
* 2.1 oz (60g) white chocolate
* 1 tbsp (15g) balsamic vinegar

* 4 tbsp (24g) almond flour

## Methods

### For the shells:

* Follow the basic macaron baking methods on pages 8–11.
* Pipe the macarons into square shapes.
* Bake at 300 °F (150 °C) for 12 minutes. Let the macaron shells cool before removing them from the baking sheet.

### For the filling:

* Chop the white chocolate, and put it in a mixing bowl.
* In a small pot, bring the cream to a boil.
* Pour over the chocolate, and add the balsamic vinegar.
* Mix together with an immersion blender until smooth.
* Transfer into a small gratin dish, and cover with cling wrap touching the ganache. Place in the refrigerator for 1 hour until the ganache hardens.
* Roast the almond flour in a pan over medium heat until fragrant and golden in color. Set aside.
* Pipe the macarons. Roll the piped macarons in the roasted almond flour. Place in a tight container before putting them in the refrigerator.
* Remove macarons from the fridge about an hour before serving in order to enjoy the fullest flavor.

Makes 24 macaron shells of 1 1/2 inches (4cm)
Preparation : 30 minutes drying time
Cooking time : 12–15 minutes baking time + 30 minutes to prepare the filling

## Ingredients

### For the shells:

* 1 egg white (40g)
* 2 1/2 tbsp (30g) superfine sugar

* 1/3 cup + 4 tsp (50g) powdered sugar
* 1/3 cup (30g) almond flour
* 1/4 tsp green food coloring powder

### For the filling:

* 3 1/2 tbsp (50g) heavy cream (35% fat)
* 1.75 oz (50g) dark chocolate (finely chopped)
* 1 drop mint extract
* 1 pinch of fleur de sel (see glossary pages 198–199)

## Methods

### For the shells:

* Follow the basic macaron baking methods on pages 8–11.
* Bake at 300 °F (150 °C) for 12 minutes. Let the macaron shells cool down before removing them from the baking sheet.

### For the filling:

* Melt the chocolate in a heat-proof bowl over a water bath.
* Bring the cream to a boil in a small pot.
* Pour it over the chocolate, mix well, and then add pinch of fleur de sel and mint flavoring.
* Transfer into a small gratin dish, and cover with cling wrap touching the ganache. Place in the refrigerator for 1 hour until the ganache hardens.

Makes 24 macaron shells of 1 1/2 inches (4cm)
Preparation : 30 minutes drying time
Cooking time : 12–15 minutes baking time + 45 minutes to prepare the filling

## Ingredients

### For the shells:

* 1 egg white (40g)
* 2 1/2 tbsp (30g) superfine sugar

* 1/3 cup + 4 tsp (50g) powdered sugar
* 1/3 cup (30g) almond flour
* 1/4 tsp blue food coloring powder

* dried cornflower petals (see glossary pages 198–199)

### For the filling:

* 1 egg yolk
* 1/4 cup (60g) butter (cubed, room temperature)
* 2 tbsp (25g) sugar
* 1 1/2 tsp (8g) water
* 1 1/2 tbsp (20g) Muscat wine (see glossary pages 198–199)

## Methods

### For the shells:

* Follow the basic macaron baking methods on pages 8–11.
* Sprinkle some cornflower petals over the piped shells.
* Bake at 300 °F (150 °C) for 12 minutes. Let the macaron shells cool down before removing them from the baking sheet.

### For the filling:

* Warm the sugar and water in a small pot over medium heat.
* Start beating the egg yolk with a hand mixer in a mixing bowl when the syrup temperature reaches 237 °F (114 °C).
* Once the sugar reaches 245 °F (118 °C), remove from the heat, and slowly pour down the side of the bowl while beating the egg yolk at medium speed.
* Keep the mixer turning until the syrup has cooled to lukewarm temperature.
* Add the butter one piece at a time, and beat until well incorporated after each addition.
* When the butter is fully incorporated, add the Muscat wine, and beat again until a smooth buttercream is obtained.
* Fill the macaron shells, and chill in the refrigerator.

Makes 24 macaron shells of 1 1/2 inches (4cm)
Preparation : 30 minutes drying time
Cooking time : 12–15 minutes baking time + 20 minutes to prepare the filling

## Ingredients

### For the shells:

* 1 egg white (40g)
* 2 1/2 tbsp (30g) superfine sugar

* 1/3 cup + 4 tsp (50g) powdered sugar
* 1/3 cup (30g) almond flour

* 1/4 tsp green food coloring powder
* 1/4 tsp red food coloring powder

### For the filling:

* 1.75 oz (50g) dark chocolate (finely chopped)
* 2 1/2 tbsp (40g) heavy cream (35% fat)
* 2 tsp (10g) extra virgin olive oil
* black olives

## Methods

### For the shells:

* Blend the almond flour and icing sugar.
* Fold the dry and wet ingredients together roughly, and scoop 1 tbsp of the mixture into a small bowl. Add the red food coloring powder, and mix until smooth and shiny.
* Add in the green food coloring powder to the main mixing bowl, and fold.
* Pipe the mixture. To draw the small heart on the piped shells, dip a chopstick into the red mixture, and drag it across the top of the piped shells to draw the heart.
* Bake at 300 °F (150 °C) for 12 minutes. Let the macaron shells cool down before removing them from the baking sheet.

### For the filling:

* Chop the pitted black olives.
* Melt the chocolate in a heat-proof bowl over a water bath.
* Put the cream in a pot, and warm it up over medium heat.
* Pour 1/3 of the cream mixture over the melted chocolate, stir, and mix. Repeat twice.
* Add the olive oil, and mix well with a hand whisk until everything is incorporated.
* Transfer to a small bowl, and let cool to room temperature. Cover with cling wrap touching the ganache, and place it in the refrigerator for 1–2 hours to harden.
* Pipe the ganache onto a shell, put a piece of black olive on top, and close with another shell.
* Fill the macaron shells and enjoy!

Olive Noir :
Black Olive & Dark Chocolate

Makes 24 macaron shells of 1 1/2 inches (4cm)
Preparation : 30 minutes drying time
Cooking time : 12–15 minutes baking time + 45 minutes to prepare the filling

## Ingredients

### For the shells:

* 1 egg white (40g)
* 2 1/2 tbsp (30g) superfine sugar

* 1/3 cup + 4 tsp (50g) powdered sugar
* 1/3 cup (30g) almond flour
* 1/4 tsp yellow food coloring

* orange food coloring

### For the filling:

* 1/4 tsp saffron
* 1.75 oz (50g) white chocolate (finely chopped)
* 2 tbsp (30g) heavy cream (35% fat)

## Methods

### For the shells:

* Follow the basic macaron baking methods on pages 8–11.
* Bake at 300 °F (150 °C) for 12 minutes. Let the macaron shells cool before removing them from the baking sheet.
* Once the shells are baked, moisten a small brush, dip it into the orange food coloring, and paint on the shells.

### For the filling:

* Warm the cream lightly, and infuse it with saffron. Leave aside for about 10 minutes.
* Melt the chocolate over a water bath.
* Drain the cream mixture over a sieve, and rewarm it over medium heat.
* Pour it over the chocolate 3 times, mixing well after each addition.
* Transfer into a small bowl, and let cool in the refrigerator for 2 hours.

Makes 24 macaron shells of 1 1/2 inches (4cm)
Preparation : 30 minutes drying time
Cooking time : 12–15 minutes baking time + 45 minutes to prepare the filling

## Ingredients

### For the shells:

* 1 egg white (40g)
* 2 1/2 tbsp (30g) superfine sugar

* 1/3 cup + 4 tsp (50g) powdered sugar
* 1 1/2 tbsp (10g) almond flour
* 2 tbsp (20g) hazelnuts
* 1/4 tsp unsweetened cocoa powder

* crushed hazelnuts

### For the filling:

* 1 1/2 tbsp (20g) hazelnuts (finely grated)
* 2 1/2 tbsp (40g) heavy cream (35% fat)
* 1.4 oz (40g) white chocolate (finely chopped)

## Methods

### For the shells:

* Blend the almond flour, hazelnuts, powdered sugar, and cocoa powder.
* Sprinkle some crushed hazelnuts over the piped shells.
* Bake at 300 °F (150 °C) for 12 minutes. Let the macaron shells cool down before removing them from the baking sheet.

### For the filling:

* Melt the chocolate in a heat-proof bowl over a water bath. Remove from the heat when half of it is melted.
* Warm the cream and grated hazelnuts in a pot over medium heat, stirring constantly.
* Pour the mixture over the melted chocolate, and mix well with a hand whisk. Pour into a small bowl, and let cool to room temperature before filling the shells.

Makes 24 macaron shells of 1 1/2 inches (4cm)
Preparation : 30 minutes drying time
Cooking time : 12–15 minutes baking time + 45 minutes to prepare the filling

The title is vertical on the left side.

## Ingredients

### For the shells:

* 1 egg white (40g)
* 1/3 cup + 4 tsp (50g) powdered sugar
* 1/3 cup (30g) ground almonds
* 2 1/2 tbsp (30g) superfine sugar
* 1/2 tsp black food coloring powder

* 1/4 tsp metallic white food coloring powder

### For the filling:

* 1 egg yolk
* 1 tbsp (15g) superfine sugar
* 1/2 cup (125g) mascarpone cheese
* 2 rolls licorice chewy candy (1.5 oz [50g])

## Methods

### For the shells:

* Follow the basic macaron methods on pages 8–11.
* Sprinkle the metallic food coloring over the piped shells.
* Bake at 300 °F (150 °C) for 12 minutes. Let the macaron shells cool down before removing them from the baking sheet.

### For the filling:

* Cut the licorice candies into small pieces.
* Whisk the egg yolk and sugar in a small bowl.
* Add half of the mascarpone cheese into the mixing bowl, and whisk until it is well mixed. Then, add the other half, and whisk again until you get a smooth cream.
* Add licorice candies, and mix lightly. Leave it in the refrigerator to set for 2 hours before piping onto the shells.

Réglisse :
Licorice Mascarpone

Makes 24 macaron shells of 1 1/2 inches (4cm)

Preparation : 30 minutes drying time

Cooking time : 12–15 minutes baking time + 30 minutes to prepare the filling

## Ingredients

### For the shells:

* 2 egg whites (80g)
* 1/3 cup (60g) superfine sugar

* 3/4 cup + 4 tsp (100g) powdered sugar
* 2/3 cup (60g) almond flour

* 1 tsp yellow food coloring
* 1 tsp green food coloring
* 1 tsp red food coloring

### For the filling:

* 5 sour candies
* 1 tbsp water
* 1.75 oz (50g) white baking chocolate (finely chopped)
* 4 tsp (40g) heavy cream

## Methods

### For the shells:

* Please follow the instructions on pages 12–13.
* Bake at 300 °F (150 °C) for 12 minutes. Let the macaron shells cool down before removing them from the baking sheet.

### For the filling:

* Crush the candies with a mortar and pestle.
* In a small pot, melt the candies in the water. Watch closely so that they do not burn.
* When the candies are melted, add in the cream. Warm up the mixture.
* Remove the cream from the heat, pour it over the white chocolate. Mix until the chocolate is melted completely, and a smooth texture is obtained.
* Let cool at room temperature, and set in the refrigerator for about 1–2 hours, checking from time to time. The ganache should be soft, but not runny.
* Fill up the shells. The macarons are best eaten the next day.

Makes 12 macaron shells of 1 1/2 inches (4cm), 12 macaron shells of 3/4 inch (2cm)
Preparation : 30 minutes drying time
Cooking time : 12–15 minutes baking time + 45 minutes to prepare the filling

## Ingredients

### For the shells:

* 1 egg white (40g)
* 1/3 cup + 4 tsp (50g) powdered sugar
* 1/3 cup (30g) ground almonds
* 2 1/2 tbsp (30g) superfine sugar

* decorating candy balls

### For the filling:

* 1 egg yolk
* 1 1/2 tbsp (30g) honey
* 1/2 cup (125g) mascarpone cheese

## Methods

### For the shells:

* Follow the basic macaron baking methods on pages 8–11.
* Pipe twelve 1.5-inch and twelve 1-inch macaron shells.
* Once baked, fill them up with the honey mascarpone cream.
* Pipe a pea-size dollop of the cream on top of the 1.5-inch shell to stick the smaller on top. Repeat to stick the decorating candy ball to the small macaron.
* Bake at 300 °F (150 °C) for 12 minutes. Let the macaron shells cool down before removing them from the baking sheet.

### For the filling:

* Whisk the egg yolk and honey until pale.
* Add half of the mascarpone into the mixing bowl, and whisk until it is well mixed. Then, add in the other half, and whisk again until you get a smooth cream.
* Leave it in the refrigerator for 2 hours to set before piping onto the shells.

Makes 24 macaron shells of 1 1/2 inches (4cm)
Preparation : 30 minutes drying time
Cooking time : 12–15 minutes baking time + 1 hour to prepare the filling

## Ingredients

### For the shells:

* 1 egg white (40g)
* 2 1/2 tbsp (30g) superfine sugar

* 1/3 cup + 4 tsp (50g) powdered sugar
* 1/3 cup (30g) almond flour
* 1/2 tsp purple food coloring powder
* 1/2 tsp lavender buds

* lavender flower buds (to sprinkle)

### For the filling:

* 1 egg yolk
* 1/4 cup (60g) butter (cubed, room temperature)
* 2 tbsp (25g) sugar
* 1 1/2 tsp (8g) water

## Methods

### For the shells:

* Follow the basic macaron baking methods on pages 8–11.
* Sprinkle 2–3 lavender buds over the piped shell before putting them in the oven. (Do not use too many lavender buds because the fragrance can be quite overwhelming).
* Bake at 300 °F (150 °C) for 12 minutes. Let the macaron shells cool down before removing them from the baking sheet.

### For the filling:

* Warm the sugar and water in a small pot over medium heat.
* Using a candy thermometer, check temperature of syrup until it reaches 237 °F (114 °C). Start beating the egg yolk in a mixing bowl.
* When the syrup temperature reaches 245 °F (118 °C), remove from the heat, and slowly pour down the side of the mixing bowl while mixing using low speed to prevent spurting.
* Keep the mixer turning, and increase the speed once all sugar syrup is poured into the bowl. Continue mixing until the mixture has cooled down to lukewarm temperature. Add in the butter one piece at a time, beating and incorporating well after each addition.
* When the butter is fully incorporated, refrigerate 10 minutes before transferring into a piping bag to fill the shells.

Makes 24 macaron shells of 1 1/2 inches (4cm)
Preparation : 30 minutes drying time
Cooking time : 12–15 minutes baking time + 1 hour to prepare the filling

## Ingredients

### For the shells:

* 1 egg white (40g)
* 2 1/2 tbsp (30g) superfine sugar

* 1/3 cup (30g) almond flour
* 1/3 cup + 4 tsp (50g) powdered sugar
* 1 tsp (5g) unsweetened cocoa powder

* cinnamon cookie (crushed)

### For the filling:

* 2 oz (50g) of cinnamon cookie (crushed into a powder in a blender)
* 1 tbsp (20g) honey (or aloe vera syrup)
* 2 1/2 tsp (10g) sugar
* 2 tbsp (30g) soy milk
* 1 oz (30g) white chocolate (finely chopped)

## Methods

### For the shells:

* Blend the almond flour, powdered sugar, and cocoa powder. Pass through a sieve, and set aside.
* Follow the instructions on pages 8–11.
* Sprinkle some crushed cinnamon cookie crumbs over the piped shells before baking in the oven.
* Bake at 300 °F (150 °C) for 12 minutes. Let the macaron shells cool down before removing them from the baking sheet.

### For the filling:

* In a small pot, warm the soy milk, sugar, and honey, but do not let it boil.
* Mix the cinnamon cookie crumbs and chocolate in a bowl.
* When the milk mixture is warm, pour in 1/3 of it into a bowl, mix well, and repeat until the mixture is used up and a smooth paste is formed.
* The mixture will be a bit runny when warm, but it will harden up slightly as it cools.
* Pour it into a jam pot, close the lid, and let it cool. Once cooled, place in the refrigerator overnight.

Makes 24 macaron shells of 1 1/2 inches (4cm)

Preparation : 30 minutes drying time

Cooking time : 12–15 minutes baking time + 1 hour to prepare the filling

## Ingredients

### For the shells:

* 1 egg white (40g)
* 2 1/2 tbsp (30g) superfine sugar

* 1/3 cup + 4 tsp (50g) powdered sugar
* 1/3 cup (30g) ground almonds

* 1/2 tsp violet coloring

* crystalized violet petals (crushed)

### For the filling:

* 3 1/2 tbsp (50g) heavy cream (35% fat)
* 1.75 oz (50g) dark baking chocolate (finely chopped)
* 1/2 tsp crushed violet petals
* 1 tsp violet syrup

## Methods

### For the shells:

* Please follow the multi-color macaron methods on pages 12–13.
* Sprinkle some crystalized violet petals over the shells before baking.
* Bake at 300 °F (150 °C) for 12 minutes. Let the macaron shells cool down before removing them from the baking sheet.

### For the filling:

* Warm the cream over medium heat.
* Meanwhile, melt the chocolate in a heat-proof bowl over a water bath.
* When the cream is warm, pour it over the chocolate and mix well.
* Add the crystalized violet petals and violet syrup into the ganache. Mix well. Let cool in the refrigerator for about 1 hour. The ganache should be soft.
* Pipe the ganache onto the macaron shells.

Makes 24 macaron shells of 1 1/2 inches (4cm)
Preparation : 30 minutes drying time
Cooking time : 12–15 minutes baking time + 1 hour to prepare the filling

## Ingredients

### For the shells:

* 1 egg white (40g)
* 2 1/2 tbsp (30g) superfine sugar

* 1/3 cup + 4 tsp (50g) powdered sugar
* 1/3 cup (30g) ground almonds
* 1/4 tsp white food coloring powder
* 1/2 tsp red food coloring
* 1/4 tsp black food coloring

### For the filling:

* 4 tsp (20g) heavy cream (35% fat)
* 1.75 oz (50g) dark baking chocolate (finely chopped)
* 2 drops of poppy flavoring

## Methods

### For the shells:

* Follow the basic macaron baking methods on pages 8–11.
* Separate 2 tbsp of the mixture, and add red food coloring, mixing well. Separate out 1 tsp of the mixture, and add black food coloring, mixing well.
* Pipe the macaron shells. Once done, dip a chopstick into the red mixture, and draw the flowers on the shells. Repeat until all shells are decorated.
* Dip a toothpick into the black mixture, and draw the dots over the flowers.
* Bake at 300 °F (150 °C) for 12 minutes. Let the macaron shells cool down before removing them from the baking sheet.

### For the filling:

* Warm the cream over medium heat.
* Meanwhile, melt the chocolate in a heat-proof bowl over a water bath.
* When the cream is warm, pour it over the chocolate, and mix well.
* Add the poppy flavoring to the ganache, and mix well. Let cool in the refrigerator for about 1 hour.
* Pipe the ganache onto the macaron shells.

# Licorice Choc :

## Licorice Candy & White Chocolate Ganache

Makes 24 macaron shells of 1 1/2 inches (4cm)
Preparation : 30 minutes drying time
Cooking time : 12–15 minutes baking time + 1 hour to prepare the filling

## Ingredients

### For the shells:

* 1 egg white (40g)
* 2 1/2 tbsp (30g) superfine sugar

* 1/3 cup + 4 tsp (50g) powdered sugar
* 1/3 cup (30g) almond flour
* 1/4 tsp black + 1/4 tsp purple food coloring powder

* 1/4 tsp gold metallic food coloring powder

### For the filling:

* 1 1/2 tbsp (25g) heavy cream (35% fat)
* 1.75 oz (50g) white chocolates (finely chopped)
* 4 hard licorice candies (crushed in a mortar and pestle)
* 1/3 cup (75g) very cold heavy cream (put in the freezer for 10 minutes)

## Methods

### For the shells:

* Follow the basic macaron baking methods on pages 8–11.
* When the macarons are baked, moisten a brush, and dip it into the gold metallic food coloring powder.
* Brush over the center of the shells gently.
* Bake at 300 °F (150 °C) for 12 minutes. Let the macaron shells cool down before removing them from the baking sheet.

### For the filling:

* Melt the chocolate in a heat-proof bowl over a water bath.
* In another pot, boil the cream with the licorice candies. Pour it over the melted chocolate 3 times.
* Incorporate the mixture, and let it cool to lukewarm temperature.
* Pour the very cold cream over the ganache, and whip it with an electric beater until it becomes fluffy.
* Refrigerate the ganache for 1–2 hours until hardened.

# salé

# {savory}

Makes 24 macaron shells of 1 1/2 inches (4cm)
Preparation : 30 minutes drying time
Cooking time : 12–15 minutes baking time + 30 minutes to prepare the filling

## Ingredients

### For the shells:

* 1 egg white (40g)
* 2 1/2 tbsp (30g) superfine sugar

* 1/3 cup + 4 tsp (50g) powdered sugar
* 1/3 cup (30g) almond flour

* a few drops of liquid blue food coloring (or mix 1/4 tsp blue food coloring powder with a few drops of water)

### For the filling:

* 3 1/2 tbsp (50g) heavy cream (35% fat)
* 2 1/2 tbsp (20g) blue cheese

* 1/2 cup (125mL) sweet wine (Muscat wine or port) (see glossary pages 198–199)
* 1/4 tsp agar-agar powder

## Methods

### For the shells:

* Blend the almond flour and powdered sugar.
* Fold the mixture following the basic macaron baking method on pages 5–7.
* Pipe the macarons in the form of rain drops: Press the piping bag, and then release the pressure while dragging down to make a pointed end.
* Dip a small brush into the food coloring and paint the piped shells.
* Bake at 300 °F (150 °C) for 12 minutes. Let the macaron shells cool down before removing them from the baking sheet.

### For the filling:

* Heat the wine and agar-agar powder in a small pot. Bring it to a boil for 2 minutes while stirring constantly.
* Pour it onto a flat plate, and let it cool to room temperature before refrigerating it to set.
* Crush the cheese in a small bowl. Add in the cream, and continue crushing any small pieces of cheese in the bowl until everything is well mixed.
* Put the bowl with the mixture in the freezer for 2 minutes.
* Whip it until the mixture reaches the consistency of whipped cream.
* Cut the wine and agar-agar jelly into small squares.
* Fill one macaron shell, add wine jelly on top, place a pea-size filling over it, and close with another shell. Put in the refrigerator.
* These macarons are best eaten within 4–6 hours because the filling tends to soak the shells if kept for too long.

Makes 24 macaron shells of 1 1/2 inches (4cm)
Preparation : 30 minutes drying time
Cooking time : 12–15 minutes baking time + 30 minutes to prepare the filling

## Ingredients

### For the shells:

* 1 egg white (40g)
* 2 1/2 tbsp (30g) superfine sugar

* 1/3 cup + 4 tsp (50g) powdered sugar
* 1/3 cup (30g) almond flour
* 1/2 tsp orange food coloring powder

### For the filling:

* 3 1/2 tbsp (50g) heavy cream (35% fat)
* 1 oz (30g) Munster French cheese (see glossary pages 198–199)
* honey (pine or eucalyptus)

## Methods

### For the shells:

* Blend the almond flour, powdered sugar, and food coloring.
* Follow the basic macaron methods on pages 8–11.
* Bake at 300 °F (150 °C) for 12 minutes. Let the macaron shells cool down before removing them from the baking sheet.

### For the filling:

* Crush the cheese in a small bowl.
* Add the cream, and continue crushing any small pieces of cheese in the bowl until everything is well mixed.
* Put the bowl with the mixture in the freezer for 2 minutes.
* Whip it up until the mixture reaches the consistency of whipped cream.
* Fill one macaron shell, add in a small amount of honey, and close it up with another shell.
* Put the filled macarons in the refrigerator.
* These macarons are best eaten within 4–6 hours because the filling tends to soak the shells if kept for too long.

Makes 24 macaron shells of 1 1/2 inches (4cm)
Preparation : 30 minutes drying time
Cooking time : 12–15 minutes baking time + 30 minutes to prepare the filling

## Ingredients

### For the shells:

* 1 egg white (40g)
* 2 1/2 tbsp (30g) superfine sugar

* 1/3 cup + 4 tsp (50g) powdered sugar
* 1/3 cup (30g) almond flour
* 1/4 tsp red food coloring powder

* metallic gold food coloring powder

### For the filling:

* 3 1/2 tbsp (50g) heavy cream (35% fat)
* 2 slices smoked salmon (cut into rectangular strips)

## Methods

### For the shells:

* Blend the almond flour, powdered sugar, and food coloring powder in the blender.
* Follow the basic macaron methods on pages 8–11.
* Bake at 300 °F (150 °C) for 12 minutes. Let the macaron shells cool down before removing them from the baking sheet.
* When the shells are baked, moisten the brush, dip it in the metallic food coloring, and paint the shells.

### For the filling:

* Place the cream in the refrigerator to make sure it stays cold.
* Place the whipping bowl and whipping blades in the freezer for an hour.
* Bring the whipping bowl out of freezer, and pour the cold cream into it. Whip it up immediately until a fluffy whipped cream is obtained.
* Fill one macaron shell with whipped cream, place a strip of smoked salmon on top, and close it up with another shell.
* Store in an airtight container in the refrigerator.
* These macarons are best eaten within 4–6 hours because the filling tends to soak the shells if kept for too long.

Makes 24 macaron shells of 1 1/2 inches (4cm)
Preparation : 30 minutes drying time
Cooking time : 12–15 minutes baking time + 30 minutes to prepare the filling

## Ingredients

### For the shells:

* 1 egg white (40g)
* 2 1/2 tbsp (30g) superfine sugar

* 1/3 cup (40g) powdered sugar
* 1/3 cup + 1 tbsp (40g) almond flour
* 1/2 tsp orange food coloring powder
* 1/4 tsp turmeric
* pinch of salt

* mustard seeds

### For the filling:

* 2 oz (60g) canned tuna in water
* 1 tbsp (14g)olive oil
* 2 tbsp coconut cream
* 1/4 tsp turmeric
* 1/4 tsp ginger powder
* 1/4 tsp of garam masala
  (see glossary pages 198–199)
* salt and pepper to taste

## Methods

### For the shells:

* Blend the almond flour, powdered sugar, food coloring, salt, and turmeric.
* Sprinkle some mustard seeds on the piped shells.
* Bake at 300 °F (150 °C) for 12 minutes. Let the macaron shells cool down before removing them from the baking sheet.

### For the filling:

* Drain tuna and press it through a sieve to remove any excess liquid.
* Crush it up lightly with a fork and blend it with all the other ingredients.
* Mix it up until smooth.
* Fill the macarons 1–2 hours before serving to prevent the macaron shells from softening up and becoming soggy from the filling.

Makes 24 macaron shells of 1 1/2 inches (4cm)
Preparation : 30 minutes drying time
Cooking time : 12–15 minutes baking time + 25 minutes to prepare the filling

## Ingredients

### For the shells:

* 1 egg white (40g)
* 2 1/2 tbsp (30g) superfine sugar

* 1/3 cup + 4 tsp (50g) powdered sugar
* 1 1/2 tbsp (10g) almond flour
* 1/4 cup (20g) pecans
* 1/4 tsp unsweetened cocoa powder
* pinch of salt

* crushed pecans

### For the filling:

* 3 tbsp (30g) bread crumbs
* 2 tbsp (20g) water
* 1 tbsp (10g) onion
* 1 tbsp (14g) olive oil
* 3.5 oz (100g) chanterelle mushrooms
* salt and pepper to taste

## Methods

### For the shells:

* Blend the almond flour, pecans, cocoa powder, and powdered sugar.
* Bake following the basic macaron baking methods on pages 8–11.
* When the shells are piped, sprinkle some crushed pecans over them.

### For the filling:

* Soak the bread crumbs in a bowl with the water.
* Chop the onion finely, and clean the mushrooms.
* Heat up the olive oil in a pan over medium heat.
* Add the mushrooms and salt and pepper to taste. Stir and cook for about 5 minutes. Let it cool to room temperature.
* Blend the cooked mushrooms and softened bread crumbs until a smooth paste is obtained.
* Fill the macaron shells. These are best eaten within 6–8 hours because the shells tend to soften up and lose their texture if left for longer.

Makes 24 macaron shells of 1 1/2 inches (4cm)
Preparation : 30 minutes drying time
Cooking time : 12–15 minutes baking time + 30 minutes to prepare the filling

## Ingredients

### For the shells:

* 1 egg white (40g)
* 2 1/2 tbsp (30g) superfine sugar

* 1/3 cup (40g) powdered sugar
* 1/3 cup + 1 tbsp (40g) almond flour
* 1/2 tsp red food coloring powder
* pinch of salt

* red metallic food coloring powder

### For the filling:

* 2 oz (60g) extra-firm organic tofu
* 2 tbsp coconut milk
* 2 tsp tom yum paste
  (see glossary pages 198–199)
* a few sprigs of cilantro leaves
* 1 tsp lime juice
* salt to taste

## Methods

### For the shells:

* Blend the almond flour, powdered sugar, food coloring, and salt.
* Follow the basic macaron baking methods on pages 8–11.
* When the macaron shells are baked, put 1/4 teaspoon of red metallic food coloring in a small bowl, wet a brush, and mix the coloring with it. Brush over the shells lightly.

### For the filling:

* Drain the tofu, and pat it dry with a paper towel. Crush it up lightly with a fork against a sieve to squeeze out any excess liquid.
* Blend it with all other ingredients.
* Mix it up until a smooth and creamy paste is obtained.
* Fill the macarons 1–2 hours before serving to prevent the macaron shells from softening up and becoming soggy from the filling.

Makes 24 macaron shells of 1 1/2 inches (4cm)
Preparation : 30 minutes drying time
Cooking time : 12–15 minutes baking time + 30 minutes to prepare the filling

## Ingredients

### For the shells:

* 1 egg white (40g)
* 2 1/2 tbsp (30g) superfine sugar

* 1/3 cup + 4 tsp (50g) powdered sugar
* 1/3 cup (30g) almond flour
* 1/2 tsp white food coloring powder

* 1/4 teaspoon red food coloring powder

### For the filling:

* half of a peeled and pitted avocado (100g)
* 1 tsp lime juice
* 2 tsp (10g) sour cream
* dash of Tabasco sauce
* salt and pepper
  (to taste)

## Methods

### For the shells:

* Follow the basic macaron baking methods on pages 8–11.
* Scoop out 2 tbsp of the folded mixture into a small bowl, add in the red food coloring, and mix well.
* Pipe the macaron shells. Once done, using a toothpick, dip into the red mixture and draw lines on the piped shells so that they look like baseballs.
* Bake at 300 °F (150 °C) for 12 minutes. Let the macaron shells cool down before removing them from the baking sheet.

### For the filling:

* Chop the avocados, and blend with the other ingredients until smooth.
* Fill the macarons 2 hours prior to serving to avoid soggy shells caused by the filling.

Makes 24 macaron shells of 1 1/2 inches (4cm)
Preparation : 30 minutes drying time
Cooking time : 12–15 minutes baking time + 30 minutes to prepare the filling

## Ingredients

### For the shells:

* 1 egg white (40g)
* 2 1/2 tbsp (30g) superfine sugar

* 1/3 cup + 4 tsp (50g) powdered sugar
* 1/4 cup (20g) almond flour
* 1 tbsp (10g) white sesame seeds
* pinch of salt

### For the filling:

* 2 oz (60g) cashews
* 2 tbsp (30g) rice milk/soy milk
* 1 tbsp (10g) white sesame seeds
* nori seaweed sheet
  (torn into small pieces)
* salt to taste

## Methods

### For the shells:

* Blend the almond flour, sesame seeds, powdered sugar, and salt.
* Follow the basic macaron methods on pages 8–11.
* Bake at 300 °F (150 °C) for 12 minutes. Let the macaron shells cool down before removing them from the baking sheet.

### For the filling:

* Blend all the ingredients to form a paste.
* Fill one macaron shell with the cashew paste, and place a small piece of the torn nori seaweed on top before closing it with another shell.
* Fill the macarons 1–2 hours before serving to prevent the shells from becoming soggy.

Nori :
Nori Seaweed, Cashews & Sesame Seeds

Makes 24 macaron shells of 1 1/2 inches (4cm)
Preparation : 30 minutes drying time
Cooking time : 12–15 minutes baking time + 30 minutes to prepare the filling

## Ingredients

### For the shells:

* 1 egg white (40g)
* 2 1/2 tbsp (30g) superfine sugar

* 1/3 cup + 4 tsp (50g) powdered sugar
* 1/4 cup (20g) almond flour
* 1/2 tsp green food coloring powder

* flax seeds (to sprinkle)

### For the filling:

* 3 1/2 cups (75g) arugula
* 1/3 cup + 1 tbsp (40g) ground hazelnuts
* 0.9 oz (25g) goat cheese
* 1 tbsp (14g) olive oil
* 1 tbsp (14g) hazelnut oil
* salt and pepper (to taste)

## Methods

### For the shells:

* Follow the basic macaron methods on pages 8–11.
* Sprinkle some flax seeds over the piped shells before baking.
* Bake at 300 °F (150 °C) for 12 minutes. Let the macaron shells cool down before removing them from the baking sheet.

### For the filling:

* Blend all the ingredients to obtain a creamy paste.
* Fill the macarons 1–2 hours before serving to prevent the shells from becoming soggy.

*Roquette :*
*Arugula & Goat Cheese Cream*

## Agar-agar

A gelatinous substance derived from red algae. Widely used as an ingredient in desserts throughout Asia. It is a great vegetarian gelatin substitute. It is usually available from Asian grocery or health food stores.

## Chai

Chai, Tchai, or Masala chai (literally "spiced tea") is a beverage from the Indian subcontinent made by brewing tea with a mixture of aromatic Indian spices and herbs.

## Chrysanthemum

Dried yellow or white chrysanthemum flowers of the species *C. morifolium* are sometimes boiled to make a sweet drink in some parts of Asia. Dried chrysanthemum flowers can be found in Asian grocery stores.

## Cornflower Petals

Petals can be used as an ingredient in some tea blends and herbal teas. The flower petals can be added to salads for color. They can be purchased from health food stores.

## Crème de Cassis

A sweet, dark red liqueur made from black currants have been crushed and soaked in ethanol, with sugar subsequently added. Crème de cassis is a specialty of Burgundy, France.

## Dark Palm Sugar

Known as Gula Melaka in Malaysia. The taste of pure coconut palm sugar resembles that of brown sugar, with more rounded caramel and butterscotch notes with rich flavor. Can be substituted with dark brown sugar.

## Espelette Pepper

A variety of chili pepper cultivated in the French community of Espelette, Pyrénées-Atlantiques, in France.

## Garam Masala

A blend of ground spices common to northern Indian and other South Asian cuisines. Its composition varies by region. Can often be found in grocery store spice aisles.

### Hibiscus Flower

Dried hibiscus is edible and often used around the world to make a colorful tea. It can also be candied and used as a garnish. It is usually found in health food stores.

### Matcha Powder

Matcha refers to finely-milled green tea. Apart from being used in the Japanese tea ceremony, matcha is also used to flavor and dye foods. It can be purchased from health food stores.

### Munster Cheese

Not to be confused with the American Muenster cheese, Munster, or Munster-géromé, is a strong-tasting, soft cheese made mainly from milk from the Vosges, between Alsace-Lorraine and Franche-Comté in France.

### Muscat Wine

Muscat wine is made from the Muscat variety of grapes of the species *Vitis vinifera*. Their color ranges from white to near black. Muscat is known for its sweet, floral aroma.

### Pandan Leaves

Pandan leaves are used for wrapping up food prior to steaming or frying, as well as giving many South-East Asian desserts their flavor. They are usually found fresh or frozen in Asian grocery stores.

### Port

Port wine is a Portuguese fortified wine. A sweet, red dessert wine, it is available in dry, semi-dry, and white varieties.

### Szechuan Pepper

Szechuan pepper is not hot or pungent like black or white pepper or chili peppers. It can be found in Chinese groceries and some supermarkets.

### Tom Yum Paste

Tom yum paste is characterized by its distinct hot and sour flavors, often used in conjunction with fragrant herbs. It is usually made with fresh ingredients such as lemongrass, kaffir lime leaves, galangal, lime juice, and crushed chili peppers. Found in Asian grocery stores.

# INDEX

# SPECIAL THANKS

To my beloved husband, Renaud Chodkowski, and my family for all their support during my baking journey.

Skyhorse Publishing books may be purchased in bulk at special discounts for sales promotion, corporate gifts, fund-raising, or educational purposes. Special editions can also be created to specifications. For details, contact the Special Sales Department, Skyhorse Publishing, 307 West 36th Street, 11th Floor, New York, NY 10018 or info@skyhorsepublishing.com.

Skyhorse® and Skyhorse Publishing® are registered trademarks of Skyhorse Publishing, Inc.®, a Delaware corporation.

Visit our website at www.skyhorsepublishing.com.

10 9 8 7 6 5 4 3 2 1

Library of Congress Cataloging-in-Publication Data is available on file.

ISBN: 978-1-62636-211-6

Printed in China